MONDAY
21 October 1805

THE DAY OF TRAFALGAR
Ian Ribbons

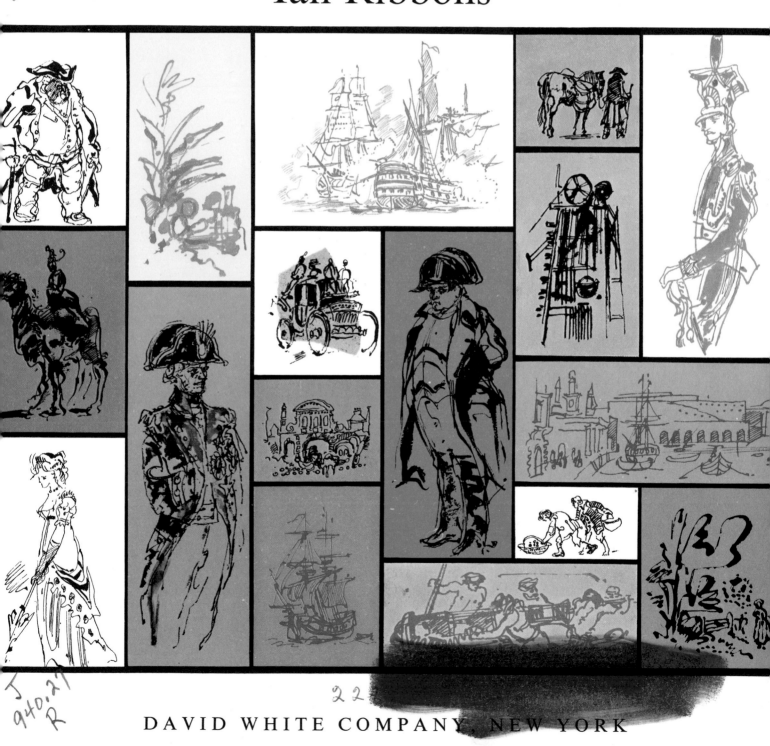

DAVID WHITE COMPANY, NEW YORK

This is the story

of one day, and of some of the actual events that
happened on it over the world.

Newspaper and other reports refer to this same
day, although published later.

Tide and coach times are from contemporary
almanacks and directories; journeys from letters
and diaries.

Published in the United States of America by David White Company, 60 East 55th Street, New York, N.Y. 10022

Library of Congress Catalog Card Number: 67-19303

PRINTED IN AUSTRIA

Night

Off the south-west coast of Spain, near Cadiz, the main combined war fleets of France and Spain struggle westwards. Head-winds make it hard going. Guns are ready for action; strained eyes watch for the blue flares and occasional flashes of gun-fire that pierce the darkness to the south. These are clearly signals from British scouting frigates to a main British fleet. The French Commander-in-Chief, Vice-Admiral Pierre Villeneuve, knows that battle is near.

Sailing also westwards, but with concealed lights, the shadowy shapes of British warships keep loose cruising order. They form the reinforced Mediterranean Squadron. Their men, too, know that battle is close. Their commander sleeps fitfully, in pain from old wounds, in his narrow cot. He is Vice-Admiral Horatio Lord Nelson, Duke of Bronte in Sicily.

Since war between Britain and France broke out again in May, 1803, Napoleon has planned the invasion of England. From the Channel ports near Boulogne 2,293 flat-bottomed boats and armed escorts would land 160,000 crack troops on the Deal beaches, and within weeks all would be over. "England will have lived," Napoleon boasted.

One condition was vital for success. Just for three days, even two, French warships must control the English Channel. Failing this, British squadrons would shatter the French troopships before they could hope to cross.

But in the North Sea, the Channel, the Atlantic, the Mediterranean, British squadrons were keeping constant watch, blockading every French and Spanish fleet in their home ports of Brest, Rochefort, Ferrol and Toulon. Napoleon was powerless until his fleets could escape.

On 27 February, 1805, orders went to French commanders at Brest and Ferrol, and to Villeneuve at Toulon, to get to sea and, avoiding battle, meet at Martinique in the West Indies. There they would join a French squadron which had escaped in a January gale from Rochefort. The combined force would then re-cross the Atlantic, storm the Channel, and shield an invasion-crossing planned for July. The whole operation depended on being able to concentrate in strength to defeat the British western squadron always on guard at Ushant.

Only Villeneuve got away. With luck he eluded Nelson, passed the Straits of Gibraltar, called out Admiral Don Federico Gravina's Spanish fleet from Cadiz, and on 9 April sailed into the Atlantic.

Night

Nelson was almost frantic with worry. Two years of patient, exhausting blockading seemed all for nothing. The main French fleet was at sea, able to make a surprise attack in any direction. "I am in truth half-dead, but what man can do to find them out shall be done," he wrote. His first fear was for Sicily or the east. For a full month he scoured the Mediterranean, often against head-winds. "I believe this ill-luck will go near to kill me," he wrote again.

At last on the 16th he heard the French had passed the Straits. At Gibraltar rumours said that they had left for the West Indies. At Cape St. Vincent the same story. On 9 May Nelson heard for sure. Waiting only for a fleet of British troopships bound for Malta to reach St. Vincent, he finally, on 12 May, sailed at top speed for Barbadoes, a month behind Villeneuve.

Napoleon's plan failed. The Brest and Ferrol fleets never got out, and the Rochefort squadron left Martinique before Villeneuve arrived. Villeneuve waited a month, then turned back for Europe, alone. By now Nelson was only 3 days' sailing behind him.

In London, invasion seemed at hand. Vice-Admiral Sir Robert Calder's British squadron fought Villeneuve in fog on 22 July, took 2 ships, but could not stop him from entering Vigo. Here fresh orders met Villeneuve: either evade the British and rush the Channel alone, or call out the French fleets still blockaded in Rochefort and Brest and fight.

Meanwhile, Nelson had reached Gibraltar on 19 July. Still finding no news of Villeneuve, he realized that an invasion of Britain could be imminent. The English Channel would now be the point of danger. On 15 August, at Ushant, Nelson joined his force with 3 other British squadrons in one great concentration to defend the western approaches.

Villeneuve did his best. He tried to refit his damaged ships at Corunna, landed his worst sick, and sailed on 13 August with a mixed and ragged force, 29 strong. He knew his only hope was to avoid battle until he could join the other French fleets. For 2 days he struggled against N.E. gales. If all else failed, his orders allowed him to retreat to Cadiz; and, finally, this he did. There his fleet was again blockaded.

And Napoleon, after waiting vainly at Boulogne, marched his Grand Army east to fight Austria and Russia, who threatened to invade France.

Nelson, ill and weak after two years constantly at sea, snatched 25 days' leave in England before he was again ordered to command the Mediterranean fleet. His flagship *Victory* brought him to Cadiz on 28 September.

To hide the strength of his fleet, Nelson placed his

main force 50 miles out to sea west of Cadiz, with a chain of cruisers watching the port. His whole aim was to draw Villeneuve out to battle. He tried starvation by blocking all merchant ships from entering the port, and he sent for fire-rockets and rocket engineers in the hope of burning the enemy out.

Napoleon himself gave the answer.

The troopships Nelson had waited for at Cape St. Vincent 4 months before had reached Malta. Russia, allied with Britain since August, had ships and soldiers at Corfu. A British force had sailed from Cork, Ireland, on 31 August. Napoleon saw his troops in Italy threatened on all sides, and ordered Villeneuve to get to sea by hook or by crook and to land troops at Naples. This then was the order that sent the combined fleet into battle.

From the 2nd to the 18th of October Villeneuve hesitated. Then he heard two things: Vice-Admiral Rosily was on his way with orders to take over his command, and 6 British ships had been seen at Gibraltar—meaning Nelson must be 6 ships short. It was now or never. The same evening Villeneuve signalled his fleet to sail.

At 7 a.m. on the 19th the inshore frigate *Sirius* flag-signalled No. 370 "Enemy is coming out of port". From ship to ship the signal passed in the growing light: Nelson, 50 miles to the west, got it at 9.30. At once he signalled "Chase, S.E." All day the British fleet sailed full speed for the Straits of Gibraltar. Dawn on Sunday the 20th found the British in position, but of the enemy no trace. In thickening weather and heavy rain-squalls Nelson stood back towards the north-west. Later the combined fleet was sighted sailing due west, apparently forced off their course by the wind. At night-fall Nelson turned away and made south-westwards; at 4 in the morning he will turn again and steer north-east.

All night long Captain Henry Blackwood, in the frigate *Euryalus*, has the most vital post in the British fleet.

Memorandum from Nelson. 20th October.
Captain Blackwood to keep with two Frigates in sight of the Enemy in the night . . .
Signals by Night.
If the Enemy are standing to the Southward, or towards the Straits, burn two blue lights together, every hour, in order to make the greater blaze. If the Enemy are standing to the Westward three guns, quick, every hour.

NELSON AND BRONTE.

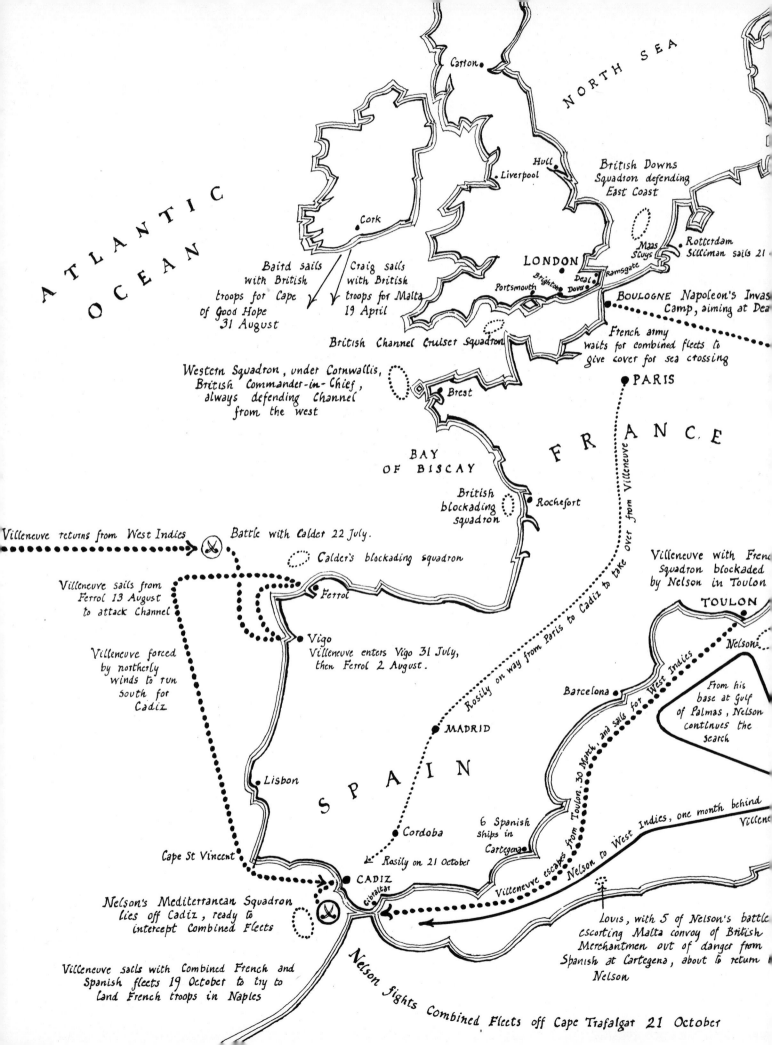

ATLANTIC OCEAN

NORTH SEA

Carton

British Downs
Squadron defending
East Coast

Hull

Liverpool

Cork

LONDON

Maas
Sluys

Rotterdam
Silliman sails 21

Brighton
Portsmouth
Deal
Dover
Ramsgate

BOULOGNE Napoleon's Invas
Camp, aiming at Dea

Baird sails
with British
troops for Cape
of Good Hope
31 August

Craig sails
with British
troops for Malta
19 April

British Channel Cruiser Squadron

French army
waits for combined fleets to
give cover for sea crossing

Western Squadron, under Cornwallis,
British Commander-in-Chief,
always defending Channel
from the west

Brest

PARIS

BAY
OF BISCAY

FRANCE

British
blockading
squadron

Rochefort

Villeneuve returns from West Indies

Battle with Calder 22 July.

Calder's blockading squadron

Villeneuve sails from
Ferrol 13 August
to attack Channel

Ferrol

Villeneuve with Frenc
Squadron blockaded
by Nelson in Toulon

TOULON

Villeneuve forced
by northerly
winds to run
south for
Cadiz

Vigo
Villeneuve enters Vigo 31 July,
then Ferrol 2 August.

Nelson

From his
base at Gulf
of Palmas, Nelson
continues the
search

Barcelona

MADRID

Lisbon

SPAIN

Cordoba

6 Spanish
ships in
Cartegena

Cape St Vincent

Rasily on 21 October

Nelson's Mediterranean Squadron
lies off Cadiz, ready to
intercept Combined Fleets

CADIZ
Gibraltar

Villeneuve sails with Combined French and
Spanish fleets 19 October to try to
land French troops in Naples

Nelson fights Combined Fleets off Cape Trafalgar 21 October

Louis, with 5 of Nelson's battle
escorting Malta convoy of British
Merchantmen out of danger from
Spanish at Cartegena, about to return
Nelson

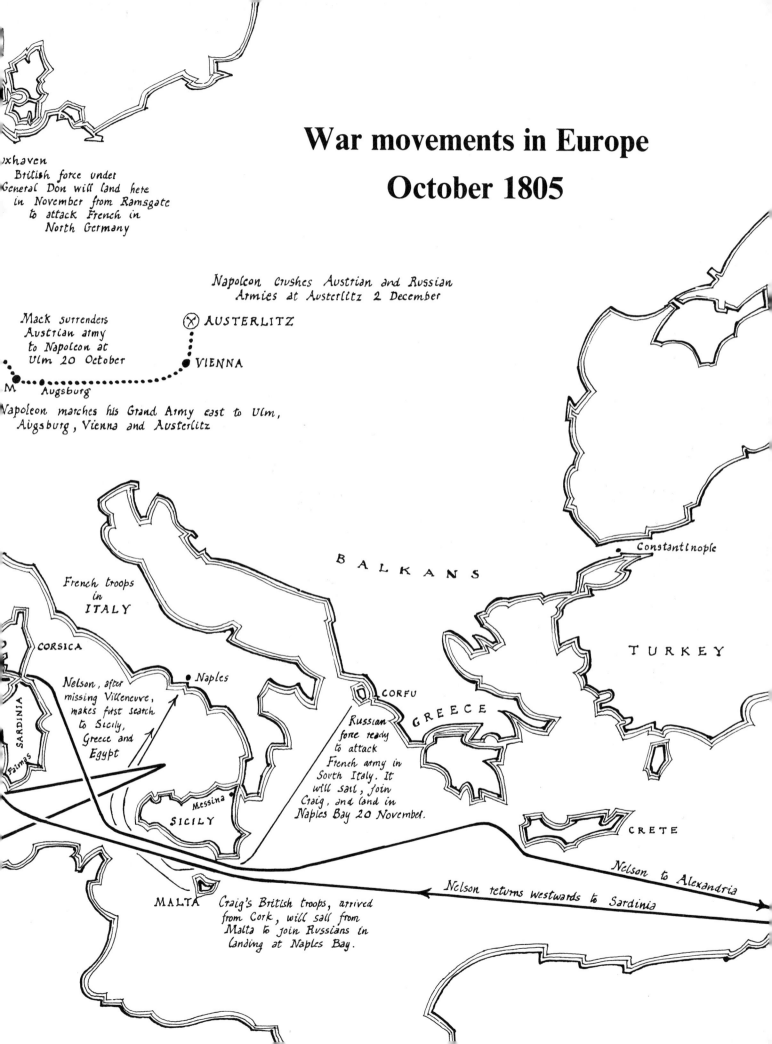

War movements in Europe
October 1805

xhaven
British force under
General Don will land here
in November from Ramsgate
to attack French in
North Germany

Napoleon crushes Austrian and Russian
Armies at Austerlitz 2 December

⊗ AUSTERLITZ

Mack surrenders
Austrian army
to Napoleon at
Ulm 20 October

● VIENNA

M ● Augsburg

Napoleon marches his Grand Army east to Ulm,
Augsburg, Vienna and Austerlitz

Constantinople

B A L K A N S

French troops
in
ITALY

CORSICA

TURKEY

Nelson, after
missing Villeneuve,
makes first search
to Sicily,
Greece and
Egypt

● Naples

CORFU

SARDINIA

G R E E C E

Palmas

Russian
force ready
to attack
French army in
South Italy. It
will sail, join
Craig, and land in
Naples Bay 20 November.

Messina ●

SICILY

C R E T E

Nelson to Alexandria

MALTA   Craig's British troops, arrived
from Cork, will sail from
Malta to join Russians in
landing at Naples Bay.

Nelson returns westwards to Sardinia

2 a.m.

CARRON, NEAR FALKIRK, SCOTLAND

Here, in the Scottish Lowlands, the sky is red from the fires of blast furnaces. Unceasingly great wooden water-wheels, 20 feet across, drive pumps which force air into the flames to make fiercer heat. The sound of hammering, wheels turning, a small army of men at work, casting and beating iron. Wherever there is coal to burn and iron-stone to quarry and an outlet to the sea, there are foundries in Britain. This, the Carron works, is the largest in Europe. A new method of boring out cannon was found here, and here the great carronades are cast, some big enough to throw a ball of 68 pounds. When mounted on the upper decks of British warships they can cause enormous damage, and are the envy and dread of the French.

JARROW, ENGLAND

Another world bustles underground in the Tyneside coalfield. In C Pit, Hebburn Colliery, the night-shift is working the High Main Seam, 770 feet below. In a gallery 3 feet high "Moon Eye" and "Gentleman Tom" crouch half-naked as they hack at the coal face. Sweat runs in white lines down their blackened faces and bodies. Behind their flickering candles the dim shapes hauling away baskets of coals are their sons of 7 and 8. Farther back, where the galleries are higher, ponies pull wagons of coal on wooden rails back to the main shaft. William Howitt visited the Durham mines as a boy. He wrote afterwards:

"In these underground regions they have ponies and asses that do not see daylight for years; and they have stables for them made of coal. What is more odd, they have abundance of rats too. . . . They are . . . so ravenous that the colliers are obliged to keep their provisions and their candles, and corn for their ponies, all in iron chests. . . . They will eat through a wooden box several inches thick in a few minutes, with their long, sharp teeth, so that there is no chance of keeping anything eatable but in iron. They keep cats too; but in spite of all this you would laugh to see a troop of rats come, while the colliers are holing, and run, and jump up at the lighted candles by which they are working, which they stick with a bit of clay to the face of the coal, and will snatch them down and scamper away in different directions with them burning in their mouths.

LONDON, ENGLAND

Horses, cattle and sheep, by the thousand, crowd the narrow streets in the northern districts of the city. By the light of flares drovers curse and beat their herds towards the great open space of Smithfield. Here, sheep are in pens, and cows and bullocks are tethered in circles with heads inwards to the centre. The noise and the torch-flames frighten the beasts and the night is filled with their bellowing. Many animals gore each other with their horns until their sides run with blood. Some will even die, trampled underfoot, before dawn. Today is the weekly Smithfield cattle-market, held on Mondays. 3,000 cattle and 16,500 lambs are recorded for today.

At the surface, thick smoke hangs over the pit-head air shaft. A crowd gathers quickly, half-dressed, with coats thrown over shoulders, to hear the dreaded news. Foremen and volunteers are lowered down the main shaft to try to dig out any miners left alive.

Newspapers are forbidden to mention mine explosions; but John Sykes of Newcastle reports today's disaster in his "Local Records". 35 men and boys are dead, leaving 25 widows and 81 children orphans.

In just 10 years' time, in this same colliery, Humphrey Davey will test his first safety lamp.

"Many a peril do these poor colliers undergo. Sometimes . . . the roof falls in; sometimes, . . . a single stroke of a pick will let in a torrent of water . . . and drown them . . ."

The most terrible danger of all is the explosive fire-damp. . . .

"Moon Eye" turns to find his candle burning with a strange brightness. He begins to shout a warning, and then a vast explosion rocks the whole mine. Pit-props collapse, men and boys scream as they are buried alive under falling rock, and all along the lower galleries one blinding sheet of flame kills men where they stand.

OYSTERS. Fresh *on Mondays,
Wednesdays, Fridays. Warehouse,
6 Sherborne Lane, back of G.P.O.
who for 55 years have served Nobility,
Gentry etc., in all parts of Kingdom,
Barrelled Oysters, Green Native Col-
chester Oysters, 5/9d barrel, from
Pyfleet, 6/9d by PETO & DAVIS.
(No oysters packed in Billingsgate,
but fresh from beds.)*

3.30 a.m.

BILLINGSGATE FISH MARKET,
LONDON, ENGLAND

The Gravesend boats have left half
an hour before. The quay is crowded
with porters and fish-wives waiting
for the incoming fleets due at 4. The
buyer from Peto's is here with a
hand-cart to collect the barrelled
oysters from the Colchester boat.
He will keep a sharp eye on the
barrels lest they be "swapped" as
they are landed.

The taverns are filled all night
with sailors, army deserters, thieves,
prostitutes as well as workmen. The
night is ugly with songs; at one inn a
sailor has drawn a knife. No one
bothers about the old night-watch-
man sheltering in his cabin. If really
necessary, someone will go for the
Bow Street Runners, who carry
pistols. Their police force has been
created only this year.

SNOW HILL, LONDON, ENGLAND

Skinner Street is all bustle and noise.
Last-minute travellers for the West
Country are jostling to get tickets
from *The Universal Coach and
Wagon Office*, at the Saracen's
Head Inn. The coachmen look at
their watches, ready to leave on the
stroke of 3.30. They wait for no one.
Their coaches are Mails, lords of the
road, superbly painted and polished,
that will shower dust from their
wheels on all they overtake. At a
steady 6 m.p.h. they are the fastest
vehicles in England.

The first Balloon coach rolls towards St. Paul's, bound for Exeter.
Others follow, for Plymouth, Falmouth, Dartmouth, Weymouth,
Dorchester, and Salisbury. Tickets
cost 2 guineas, single. Each coach
carries an armed guard on its roof.

4 a.m.

TALBOT INN, RIPLEY, ENGLAND

The Portsmouth stage-coach is
changing horses. An ostler holds
the traces while the driver adjusts
the reins in his numbed hands. The
coach left Portsmouth yesterday
evening at 6, and will take another
5 hours to cover the last 25 miles to
London. Inside the stuffy coach
2 farmers and 4 women seem asleep.

The "outside" passengers emerge
from the yard to climb up top again.
Even a mild October night is none
too warm on a coach roof, although
young men prefer it to the fug inside. One offers a nip of brandy to
the driver.

A true coachman, he doesn't
refuse. George Matcham, Nelson's
young nephew, when travelling from
Bath a month before, had asked his
coachman why a passenger was un-
well. "Ah (said he) he mix'd Milk
with his Rum in the Morning; had
he taken the Rum alone, he would

have been the better for it."

Exactly 5 weeks earlier, on
Monday, 16 September, Benjamin
Silliman, an American teacher of
chemistry on a tour of Europe, came
to London in this same coach, the
day after he had seen Nelson embark at Portsmouth. He wrote in his
diary then that 19 people squeezed
on top!

PARIS, FRANCE

In the Rue Notre Dame des Victoires, the *diligences*, run by the Service Général des Messageries, prepare to set out. The lumbering coaches carry both parcels and passengers. The 5 a.m. for Basle, Lyons and Strasbourg is loading. It leaves on uneven dates, taking $5\frac{1}{2}$ days en route.

The narrow street echoes to the cries of drivers, the cracking of whips, hooves on cobbles. Four *diligences* draw away together, at 4 a.m. The daily for Liége will take $3\frac{1}{2}$ days, the Orléans coach only 1. The Geneva *diligence* will be on the road a week, and the coach for Toulouse 8 days.

At 147, Place de l'Oratoire, the daily "Berline à six Places", a smaller and faster affair, clatters off for Rouen.

4.30 a.m.

MANCHESTER, ENGLAND

In every direction bells from 60 cotton mills are calling people to work. Figures in tattered clothes, some in wooden clogs, file through the darkness along hill-side paths to start their day. Many of them speak with southern and country accents for they have migrated to find work in the growing mills. Over the last 15 years the population has boomed from 50,000 to 95,000 in Manchester alone.

They will be standing at their frames from 5 to midday, then after an hour's break for a bread and cheese dinner, again from 1 p.m. to 8 at night. Yesterday, Sunday, they rested, but many had no heart to do anything but sleep or drink cheap gin.

They move sullenly, resigned to face another week's drudgery. They have white, sallow faces; some are crippled. Few taste milk or meat. Women earn 5/-, men up to 10/- a week. Some are fevered, driven to work by poverty. Their barren lives form the backbone of the English Industrial Revolution.

5.50 a.m.

A calm morning; the wind dropped; a ground swell running towards land. It is 46 minutes before sunrise. In the growing light the shapes of the British fleet become clearer. With each minute one can see farther across the water.

A cry, then another; then many together.

"As the day began to dawn, a man at the topmast-head called out: 'A sail on the starboard bow,' and in two or three minutes more he gave another call, that there was more than one sail, for indeed they looked like a forest of masts rising from the ocean . . ." as seaman Jack Nasty-Face, on the *Revenge*, writes later. Midshipman Badcock is on duty watch on the *Neptune*. "At the first dawn of day a forest of strange masts was seen to leeward. I ran aft and informed the officer of the watch. The Captain was on deck in a moment . . ."

An officer of the *Belleisle*: "The whole force of the enemy was discovered standing to the southward, distant about nine miles, between us and the coast near Trafalgar. I was awakened by the cheers of the crew and by their rushing up the hatchways to get a glimpse of the hostile fleet."

Vice-Admiral Cuthbert Collingwood, second in command of the fleet, is in his cabin in the *Royal Sovereign*. His servant Smith helps him dress. Smith writes later that Collingwood "during all this time, was shaving himself with a composure that quite astonished me. Admiral Collingwood dressed himself that morning with peculiar care; . . . meeting Lieutenant Clavell, 'You had better,' he said, 'put on silk stockings, as I have done: for if one should get a shot in the leg, they would be so much more manageable for the surgeon.'"

Doctor William Beatty is surgeon on Nelson's *Victory*, which flies the flag of Admiral of the White. He describes Nelson: "His Lordship came upon deck soon after daylight: he was dressed as usual in his Admiral's frock-coat, bearing on the left breast four stars of different orders, which he always wore with his common apparel. He displayed excellent spirits, and expressed his pleasure at the prospect of giving a fatal blow to the naval power of France and Spain . . ." Nelson "did not wear his sword: it had been taken

from where it hung up in his cabin, and was laid ready on his table; but he forgot to call for it. This was the only action in which he ever appeared without a sword."

6 a.m.

Within minutes of sighting the enemy, the *Victory* flag-signals to the fleet No. 72 "Form the Order of Sailing in 2 columns". The fleet, scattered after a night without lights, is to close up in 2 lines of battle. The *Victory*'s flags are lowered; immediately signal No. 76 is run up: "Bear up and sail in direction shown", together with E.N.E. flags. Frigates repeat the signals to outlying ships. Slowly the yards are braced to a new set, their sails shiver to the breeze, and, as wind and rudders begin to bite, the great ships, rolling on the swell, head round to the eastwards.

The light grows clearer. From the decks now one can make out the line of the French and Spanish fleet, stretching for 5 miles across the horizon.

9 MILES TO THE EAST

All through the night Villeneuve and Gravina, the French and Spanish Admirals, have expected attack. The British flares and gun-fire to seawards have dogged every movement of their fleet. As the last darkness pales before dawn, the French and Spanish, like the British, search anxiously for their enemy with telescopes. At 6.30 the frigate *Hermione*, an advance scout, flies the warning-signal "Enemy in sight to windward". Soon after, Captain Mahé finishes his count of the British, making it 33 sail. This, too, is signalled by the *Hermione*.

For Villeneuve and Gravina there is now no shred of doubt; battle is certain. The whole combined fleet has cleared for action during the night. The sense of nightmare, of a ghost enemy, has passed and instead the plain sight of the British fleet cheers everyone's spirits.

6.30 a.m.

9 miles westwards, the *Victory* flies its third signal of the day, No. 13, "Prepare for battle".

6.36 a.m.

CHELSEA VILLAGE, NEAR LONDON

Sunrise. The Thames on the ebb. A string of empty barges passes downstream under the wooden Battersea bridge. They are returning empty with the tide to the dung wharves at Blackfriars. They supply stable dung (at 2/- a two-ton cart-load), night soot, raw horse-bones, burnt bones and coal ashes (at 6/- a cart-load) and best soot at 8d a sack to the vegetable gardens of Kensington, Brompton, Chelsea, Fulham, and Chiswick. Others are loading at the wharves, ready to sail upstream when the tide turns at 8.

LITTON MILL, TIDESWELL, ENGLAND

Robert Blincoe, 13 years old, an orphan from St. Pancras workhouse, stands at a stretching-frame in Mr. Ellice Needham's cotton mill. He was beaten out of bed at 4.30 and has been at work since 5. His working day will finish at 10 p.m., with one break of 40 minutes for lunch. Breakfast will be brought to him in a pail at any time between 8 and 11 in the morning. He said: "On Sunday, bacon-broth and turnips were served out, which they eat with oaten-cake, in dirty wooden bowls . . . in this, rusty, half-putrid, fish-fed bacon and unpared turnips were boiled . . . there was generally a large quantity of this broth to spare . . . into this stuff, no better than hog-wash, a few pails of water were poured and some meal stirred in, and the disgusting mess served out for supper or next day's breakfast . . ."

Technically he will be an apprentice until he is 21. The apprentices sleep, locked in, 50 to a room, and are allowed soap to wash with only on Friday nights. Blincoe will have to swallow breakfast standing at the machinery, and of the 40 minutes for lunch-break 20 minutes will be spent cleaning the frames.

BULVERTON HILL, DEVON, ENGLAND

A man in light woollen drawers and flannel shirt is running down the steep hill-road near Harpford Wood, leading to Newton Poppleford and Exeter. The road curves sharply down to a bridge over the River Otter; running steadily he crosses, and disappears on the rising ground towards Exeter. He is a carpenter called Thomas Pinn.

The *Sporting Magazine* describes how he has staked £5 that he can run there from Sidmouth and back, a distance of 32 miles, in 5 hours. The paper says: "He started precisely at 6 o'clock in the morning, and arrived at the Castle Gate, Exeter, at 10 minutes before 8 . . . and returned to Sidmouth ¾ of an hour within the time allowed."

Englishmen will bet on anything.

THE CITY ROAD, LONDON

A ragged band of 7 children, from 4 to 6 years old, carrying heavy sacks, limp into London behind 2 Master Chimney Sweepers. They have come from a camp of rough huts on Finsbury Fields. They have been stolen or bought from destitute parents. Their morning's work will be to claw out soot from narrow chimneys by their own bodies, climbing in choking blackness. To force the youngest up, "pins are forced into their feet by the boy that follows them up the chimney, and lighted straw has been applied for that purpose." Their bones are already deformed, ankles and knees twisted, and some have contracted cancer of the lung. A Report in 1817 will find facts like this, and will lead to the stopping of child labour in chimneys.

DURWESTON FARM, DURWESTON, ENGLAND

A group of figures on the skyline shows dark against the sunrise. In the distant field an old ploughman tightens the traces on his 4 great Lancashire dray-horses, his fingers fumbling with the cold, tough leather. Behind the 2 pairs of horses a heavy Sull plough is harnessed. With his grandson to help him he will work until dark. In 10 hours they will, with luck, plough $\frac{3}{4}$ of an acre for winter fallows. The stubble from last summer's big harvest must be broken before the frosts of November make the ground iron-hard.

Twenty years ago he was one of 30 yeoman farmers who owned their land in Durweston. Now there are 2 large estates only, and he spends his old age as a labourer. All over England small farms have been bought up and combined under rich landowners: many yeoman farmers have emigrated or now work in factories.

NORWICH, ENGLAND

The tenth-largest city in England, and still one of the richest, has set up a work-house in the old palace of the Duke of Norfolk. Work-houses are never happy places; this is one of the worst.

550 paupers are working their weaving-frames. Outside the work-room, they have only their beds—often shared—to live, sit, eat and sleep on. The rooms are filthy, with foul air.

One 12-year-old boy carries punishment weights. James Neild, in a letter to the *Gentleman's Magazine* last month, described meeting the boy, William Raynor: "He had round his neck an iron collar called a yoke, with 4 projecting prongs, secured by a large clumsy iron padlock; . . . his neck was slightly galled; upon one leg was a strong iron ring fastened near the ankle, to which was attached a massy chain . . . at the end of this chain was a log of wood . . . weighing altogether 22 lb . . . the yoke round his neck had never been taken off during 3 weeks . . . as soon as he had finished his work, the chain and log were regularly fastened on his leg, and in that state he passed the night." This was the punishment for trying to run away. It will continue for 6 months.

ISLEWORTH, ENGLAND

A swing-cart, piled high with second-crop raspberries, is leaving the fruit gardens. The load will sell, later in the morning, at Covent Garden Market in London to distillers of cordials. 3 or 4 women, fruit pickers from Shropshire who work in the gardens, walk behind the cart. Each carries on her head a 12-gallon-basket of the last of the season's eating-raspberries. After a 10-mile-walk to Covent Garden they will sell each basket-load for 3/6d.

WROXTON ABBEY, NEAR BANBURY, ENGLAND

A gun-shot echoes across the fields, and dogs are unleashed from beside a group of men in great-coats to race after the fallen bird.

"The Earl of Guildford has a large party of sporting friends at his seat at Wroxton Abbey." *Morning Chronicle*

A straggling line of farm-labourers crunch twigs and rotting leaves underfoot as they move through the undergrowth, beating sticks and shouting as they go, to drive the birds from cover.

A crackling, a whirr of wings, and the brilliant red and brown of

a pheasant shows against the dark wood. Two more gun-shots, and again a bird drops . . .

Next Monday the first fox-hunt of the season begins.

6.40 a.m.

AT SEA, OFF CAPE TRAFALGAR

British fleet answers the signal "Prepare for action". On every ship drummers beat to quarters. In the dim light of the gun-decks, gun-crews of 10, 12 or 15 men each begin work. Port-lids are raised and the iron guns, weighing up to $2\frac{1}{2}$ tons, are run forward on massive wooden carriages to the ports. Tompions are taken from muzzles, and breeching ropes anchored to take the recoil. One gun broken loose in action can kill as many men, as it careers across the deck, as enemy gun-fire.

Tables are stowed, sleeping-hammocks stuffed in the bulwarks for protection against musket-fire. To lessen fire risk, buckets of water are placed ready to wet the canvas screens around hatchways. The decks are sprinkled well with sand to stop them becoming too slippery with blood. Master gunners unlock the powder-magazines and weigh the charge bags. A 32 lb. shot takes a third of its weight in powder. Cannon-balls are carried to the guns in hammocks. On the forecastles and poops canisters of musket-balls and scrap iron stand by the 68-pounder carronades. The slow-match, for lighting a fuse should a flintlock fail, is lit and burns over a water-barrel.

Jack Nasty-Face is on the *Revenge*: "Each ship was making the usual preparations, such as breaking the Captain's and officers' cabins, and sending all the lumber below. The doctors, parson, purser, and lob-lolly men were also busy, getting the medicine-chest and bandages out, and sails prepared for the wounded to be placed on, that they might be dressed in rotation as they were taken down to the after-cockpit. In such a bustling time . . . some would be offering a guinea for a glass of grog, whilst others were making a sort of mutual verbal will, such as: 'If one of Johnnie Crapeau's shots knocks my head off, you will take all my effects; and if you are killed and I am not, Why I will have all yours'."

2nd Lieutenant Ellis is with the Marines on the *Ajax*: "I was sent below with orders, and was much struck with the preparations made by the blue-jackets, most of whom were stripped to the waist; a handkerchief was tightly bound round their heads and over the ears, to deaden the noise of the cannon, many men being

deaf for days after an action. . . . Some were sharpening their cutlasses, others polishing the guns . . . whilst 3 or 4, as if in a mere bravado, were dancing a hornpipe; but all seemed anxious to come to close quarters with the enemy. Occasionally they would look out of the ports, and speculate as to the various ships of the enemy, many of whom had been on former occasions engaged by our vessels."

7 a.m.

The French drummers strike up the "Générale" as everywhere the order is shouted: "Branle-bas de combat!" Villeneuve signals "Form line of battle", and at 7.20 he orders "Close interval between ships". At 7 the *Victory* signals "Bear due East". At 7.50 Nelson signals for his frigate captains to come on board.

In his cabin, Nelson slowly scrawls the last thoughts he will put to paper: one is a prayer, the other an addition to his will: "I leave Emma Lady Hamilton therefore a legacy to my King and Country. . . . I also leave to the beneficence of my Country my adopted daughter, Horatia Nelson Thompson; and I desire she will use in future the name of Nelson only. These are the only favours I ask of my King and Country, at this moment when I am going to fight their Battle."

Soon after 8, Blackwood and the other frigate captains come aboard. Blackwood from the *Euryalus*, and Thomas Masterman Hardy, captain of the *Victory*, witness the will.

Nelson's one anxiety is that the enemy may escape. Climbing to the poop, he sees the lines of his fleet beginning to form; the ships are running before a light westerly breeze, with every sail set.

Ships' Logs record:

Victory "out all reef topsails, set steering sails and royals"

Orion "hove several things overboard"

Belleisle "threw overboard . . . 7 butts etc., out all reefs and made sail"

Prince "at 8, set main topmast steering sails, and all sails"

Swiftsure "all possible sails set"

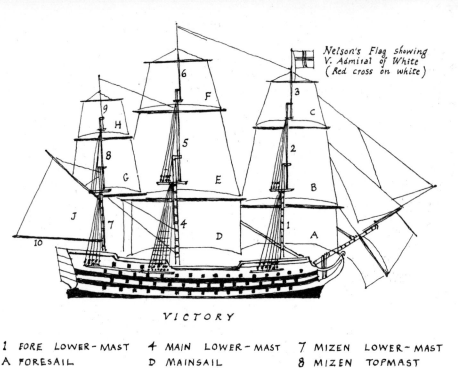

Nelson's Flag showing
V. Admiral of White
(Red cross on white)

VICTORY

1	FORE LOWER-MAST	4	MAIN LOWER-MAST	7	MIZEN LOWER-MAST
A	FORESAIL	D	MAINSAIL	8	MIZEN TOPMAST
2	FORE TOPMAST	5	MAIN TOPMAST	G	MIZEN TOPSAIL
B	FORE TOPSAIL	E	MAIN TOPSAIL	9	MIZEN TOPGALLANT MAST
3	FORE TOPGALLANT MAST	6	MAIN TOPGALLANT MAST	H	MIZEN TOPGALLANT
C	FORE TOPGALLANT	F	MAIN TOPGALLANT	10	DRIVER BOOM
				J	GAFFSAIL

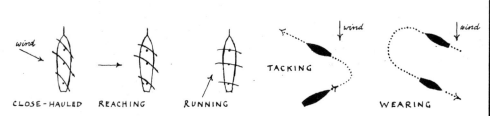

wind

CLOSE-HAULED   REACHING   RUNNING   TACKING   WEARING

wind   wind

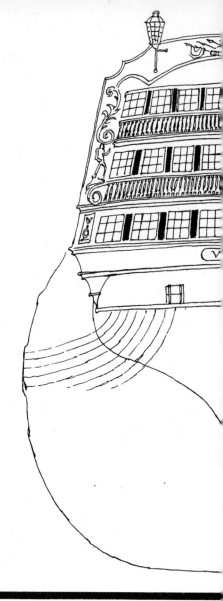

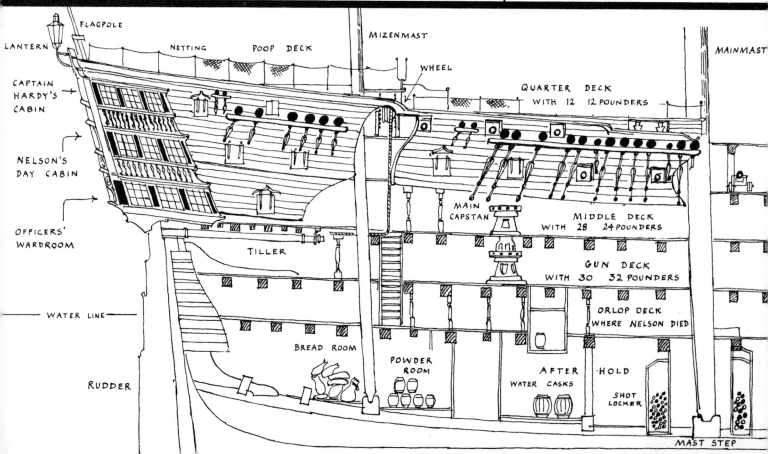

LANTERN   FLAGPOLE   NETTING   POOP DECK   MIZENMAST   MAINMAST

WHEEL

CAPTAIN HARDY'S CABIN   QUARTER DECK WITH 12 12 POUNDERS

NELSON'S DAY CABIN

MAIN CAPSTAN   MIDDLE DECK WITH 28 24 POUNDERS

OFFICERS' WARDROOM

TILLER   GUN DECK WITH 30 32 POUNDERS

ORLOP DECK WHERE NELSON DIED

WATER LINE

BREAD ROOM   POWDER ROOM   AFTER HOLD   WATER CASKS

RUDDER   SHOT LOCKER   MAST STEP

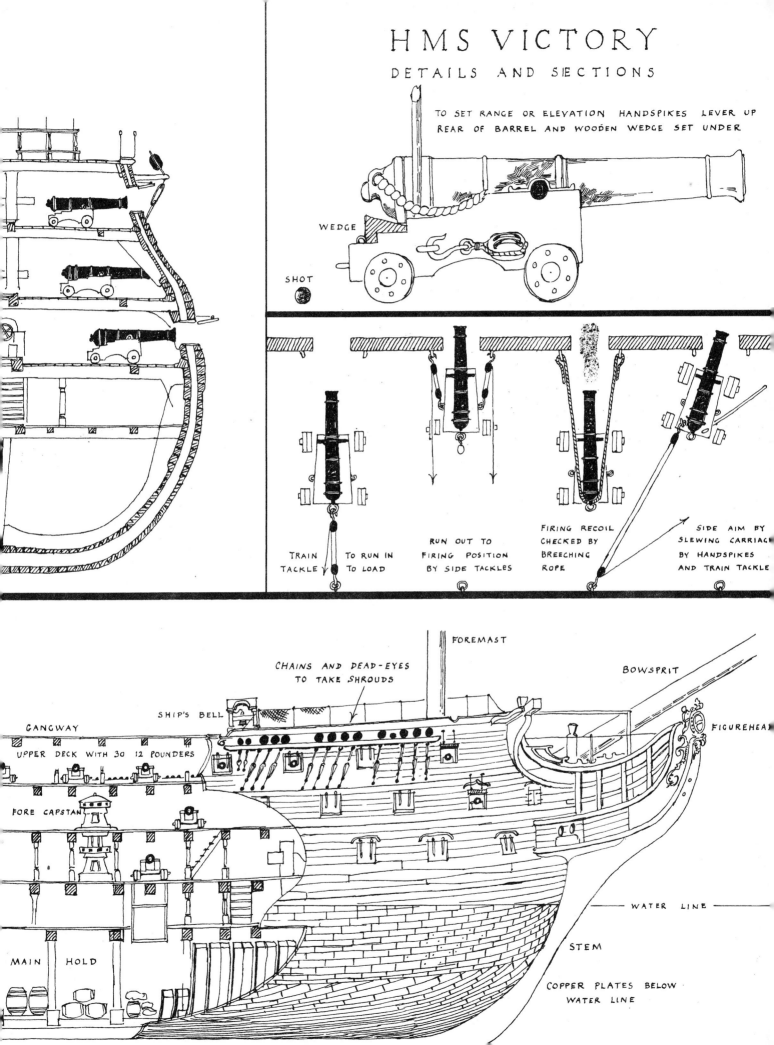

HMS VICTORY
DETAILS AND SECTIONS

TO SET RANGE OR ELEVATION HANDSPIKES LEVER UP
REAR OF BARREL AND WOODEN WEDGE SET UNDER

WEDGE

SHOT

TRAIN TACKLE · TO RUN IN TO LOAD

RUN OUT TO FIRING POSITION BY SIDE TACKLES

FIRING RECOIL CHECKED BY BREECHING ROPE

SIDE AIM BY SLEWING CARRIAGE BY HANDSPIKES AND TRAIN TACKLE

FOREMAST

CHAINS AND DEAD-EYES TO TAKE SHROUDS

BOWSPRIT

SHIP'S BELL

GANGWAY

FIGUREHEAD

UPPER DECK WITH 30 12 POUNDERS

FORE CAPSTAN

WATER LINE

STEM

MAIN HOLD

COPPER PLATES BELOW WATER LINE

8 a.m.

Winds light, opposing fleets 7 miles apart, lines still forming. At 8.20 the French and Spanish fleet is signalled to wear. Villeneuve said: "The enemy's fleet . . . seemed to be heading en masse for my rear squadron; with the double object, apparently, of engaging in greatly superior force and of cutting the Combined Fleet off from Cadiz. I therefore signalled for the fleet to wear all together, and form line of battle in reverse order."

Villeneuve knows the odds are against him. He is beset by difficulties. From the start, hopeless plans from Napoleon. Inexperienced captains, raw sailors, gunners without practice. By September last, 1731 men in hospital, 311 deserters. A fleet able to form line and little more. Nelson is a spectre, haunting his every move. Villeneuve cannot forget seeing, 7 years before, the destruction at the Battle of the Nile, when Nelson annihilated a French fleet at Aboukir Bay.

Spanish ill-feeling rose after 2 Spanish ships were lost to Calder. At Cadiz, Spanish officials refused Villeneuve stores, ignored his orders. French officers were insulted, French seamen knifed in the streets. Dumanoir and Magon, Villeneuve's Vice-Admirals, distrust him. Gravina, the Spanish Admiral, had wanted to resign. Napoleon's opinion: "Villeneuve is a wretch who ought to be broken," the Admiral can imagine.

Carefully dressed, hair powdered, the 42-year-old aristocrat from Provence stands proudly with expressionless face. He awaits his fate, whether it be victory, defeat, or death.

On the deck of the British flagship, amongst a group of captains, a slight figure stands dwarfed by a much bigger and taller man. This is Captain Hardy; the smaller figure is that of Nelson, Vice-Admiral of the White. With nerves taut, intent that this time the French shall finally be brought to action, Nelson's eye strains at a telescope. Captain Blackwood said: "He seemed very much to regret, and with reason, that the Enemy tacked to the Northward, and formed their Line on the larboard, instead of the starboard tack, which latter line of bearing would have kept the Straits' Mouth open; instead of which, by forming to the Northward, they brought the shoals of Trafalgar and St. Pedro under our lee . . ."

Horatio Nelson has served at sea since he was a boy of 12; now, at 47, he is England's idol. Crowds cheered and followed him in London. Children know his name. Without wealth or special connections, he has fought his way to the top of his profession through sheer ability.

He has lost his right arm and the sight of the right eye in action; a green shade protects his left eye, fast going blind also. His blue undress-uniform coat is faded and crumpled, its 4 stars tarnished. His face is burned brown by years at sea.

Officers are worried for Nelson's safety. Dr. Beatty "made known to Dr. Scott his fears that his Lordship would be made the object of the Enemy's marksmen, and his desire that he might be entreated by somebody to cover the stars on his coat with a handkerchief." But no one dares to suggest this, and nothing is said.

Collingwood, second in command, leads the lee division in the *Royal Sovereign*. Signals fly from his flagship: 8.45 a.m. "Make more sail". 9.20 a.m. "Make more sail". 9.40 a.m. "Make more sail".

10 a.m.

On the *Victory*, "About 10 o'clock," said Blackwood later, "Lord Nelson's anxiety to close with the Enemy became very apparent: he frequently remarked that they put a good face upon it; but always quickly added, 'I'll give them such a dressing as they never had before'." Blackwood goes on: "I proposed hoisting his Flag in the *Euryalus*, whence he could better see what was going on. . . . But he would not hear of it, and gave as his reason the force of example."

Blackwood and Hardy, still thinking of Nelson's safety, then suggest the *Victory* should keep her battle order and let other ships lead the division.

Blackwood says, that Nelson "at length consented to allow the *Téméraire*, which was then sailing abreast of the *Victory*, to go ahead, and hailed Captain Harvey . . . Captain Harvey being rather out of hail, his Lordship sent me to communicate his wishes, which I did; when, on returning . . ., I found him doing all he could to increase rather than diminish sail, so that the *Téméraire* could not pass . . ."

10.30 a.m.

Fleets 2½ miles apart. Hulls can be seen. Midshipman Badcock says: "Some of the enemy's ships were painted like ourselves—with double yellow sides, some with a broad single red or yellow streak, others all black, and the noble *Santissima Trinidada*, 138 guns, with 4 distinct lines of red."

Under the lightest of winds, the British divisions, flying every stitch of canvas, crawl forward across the water. Their speed is just under 2 miles an hour.

10.30 a.m.

AT SEA, OFF CAPE TRAFALGAR

On the gun-decks, everything nearly ready. The men are eating breakfast—a special one of beer, bread and cheese. Captains inspect the gun-crews. Some guns in the *Bellerophon* are chalked "Victory or Death".

A seaman's life is hard and brutal. Filthy food, cramped quarters and foul air below decks; rain and storms above; and pay only at the end of a voyage (perhaps lasting years), if he remains alive. An able-seaman earns £1.9.6d a month; an ordinary seaman £1.3.6d; a boy £8 a year. Out of this, they must pay for their clothes. The *Victory*'s crew totals 663 officers and seamen, not counting soldiers, or marines. It includes 22 Americans, 7 Dutchmen, 6 Swedes, 9 West Indians, and 27 others from almost every country in Europe—foreigners forced on board by press-gangs. First-class-boy Johnny Doag, from Edinburgh, is only 10. Four 12-year-old boys and six aged 13 serve mainly to carry powder to the guns.

Fresh meat and vegetables are possible only near port; many seamen carry spots and swollen gums from scurvy. Admiral Collingwood wrote, on 24 September, from the *Dreadnought*, that he had found another cause of the disease: "I think I perceive a difference in those ships which have tubes from the Fore-castle in the Bay, betwixt decks, by which the Mephitic air of the Lower Deck, during the night, passes off in great abundance, which air I believe contributes more to the scurvy . . . than either long cruizes, or want of vegetables."

Seaman Jack Nasty-Face, on the *Revenge*, joined the Navy last May. He writes: "I was ordered down to the hold, where I remained all night . . . with my companions in wretchedness, and the rats running over us in numbers. When released, we were ordered into the Admiral's tender, which was to convey us to the *Nore*.

"Upon getting on board this vessel, we were ordered down in the hold, and the gratings put over us; as well as a guard of Marines placed round the hatchway, with their muskets loaded and fixed bayonets. . . . In this place we spent the day and following night huddled

together; for there was not room to sit or stand separate; indeed, we were in a pitiable plight, for numbers of them were sea-sick, some retching, others were smoking, whilst many were so overcome by the stench, that they fainted. . . . As soon as the officer on deck understood that the men below were overcome with foul air, he ordered the hatches to be taken off, when daylight broke in upon us; and a wretched appearance we cut, for scarcely any of us were free from filth and vermin."

Seamen work in watches of 4 hours on, 4 hours off, snatching rest in their hammocks when they can. Jack writes: "At eight bells the Boatswain's Mate pipes to breakfast. This meal usually consists of burgoo, made of coarse oatmeal and water; others will have Scotch coffee, which is burnt bread boiled in some water, and sweetened with sugar.

"About eleven o'clock, or six bells, when any of the men are in irons, or on the black list, the boatswain or mate are ordered to call all hands; the culprits are then brought forward by the Master-at-Arms, . . . the Captain orders the man to strip; he is then seized to a grating by the wrists and knees; his crime is then mentioned, and the prisoner may plead; but, in nineteen cases out of twenty, he is flogged for the most trifling offence.

"After punishment, the Boatswain's Mate pipes to dinner, it being eight bells, or twelve o'clock; . . . at one bell the piper is called to play 'Nancy Dawson', or some other lively tune, a well-known signal that the grog is ready to be served out. It is the duty of the cook from each mess to fetch and serve it out to his messmates, of which every man and boy is allowed a pint, that is, one gill of rum and three of water, to which is added lemon acid, sweetened with sugar. . . . It may not be known to everyone that it is grog which pays debts, and not money, in a man-of-war."

Nelson dislikes flogging, but most captains think it the only way to keep order. Boatswains' mates practise on casks, watched by the boatswains. A captain can order flogging at the gangway for the slightest reason. At any time any officer can order the boatswain's mate to "start" a man by thrashing his back with a rope's end. As Jack says: "This punishment is so common that no minute is made of it even in the log book."

Attempted escape means court martial and "flogging round the fleet." Jack will see this at Spithead just 4 years later, in 1809: "The signal was made for a boat from each ship, with a guard of Marines, to attend the punishment. The man is placed in a launch, . . . under the care of the Master-at-Arms and a doctor. There is a capstan bar rigged fore and aft, to which this poor fellow is lashed by his wrists. . . . The cat-o'-nine-tails is applied to the bare back, and at about every six lashes a fresh Boatswain's Mate is ordered to relieve the executioner of this duty, until the prisoner has received, perhaps, twenty-five lashes. He is then cast loose, and, allowed to sit down with a blanket rolled round him, is conveyed to the next ship, escorted by this vast number of armed boats, accompanied by that doleful music, 'The Rogue's March'. In this manner he is conveyed from ship to ship, receiving alongside of each a similar number of stripes with the cat, until the sentence is completed."

10.40 a.m.

The fleets about 2 miles apart.

Captain Jean Lucas, on the French *Redoutable*, has trained men ready for boarding an enemy. He says: "I had cartridge-cases made for each of the captains of the guns, to hold two grenades apiece . . . I had a hundred muskets, fitted with long bayonets. . . . The picked men to whom these were served out were specially trained at musketry and stationed in the shrouds. All the men with cutlasses and pistols were regularly trained."

Preceded by fifes and drums, captains of the combined fleet, together with their first officers, inspect the batteries and the gunners. Villeneuve himself tours the decks of his flagship, the *Bucentaure*. Everywhere the sound of drums, of cheers, of cries of "Vive l'Empereur!"

Lt. Hoffman of the *Tonnant* says: "All our ships that had bands were playing 'Rule Britannia', 'Downfall of Paris', etc. Our own struck up 'Britons strike home'." But mostly there is silence on the British ships. Midshipman Robinson is on the *Euryalus*. "The fleet held steadfastly on its course in grim silence that was unbroken save for, now in one ship, now in another, a gruff, hoarse-toned order, short and sharp, or the chirp of a bo'sun's whistle, the creaking of a spar, or flap of a sail."

10.45 a.m.

PORTSMOUTH, ENGLAND

Early fog has lifted. A fine morning, with light breezes.

One hour to high water; ships of all kinds are still coming in on the tide. Valuable convoys of merchantmen from Jamaica and the West Indies have arrived, escorted by British warships against capture by the French. One great fleet has been split by storms, but most ships have reached the sheltered waters of the Solent, off the Isle of Wight. Newspapers report all movements in and out of port today:

"Homeward bound W. India fleet, windbound at Motherbank; Leeward Isles convoy, after 14 weeks, with 235 ships; 45 dropped off in wind with *Hyena* frigate, 187 arrived in Channel with *Illustrious*."

Many are warships: ships of the line, frigates, sloops.

"Arrived the *Melampus* frigate, Capt. Poyntz, with *Hope* smuggling lugger, laden with spirits ... captured off Lizard."

"Arrived *Nimble* cutter, Lt. Delaphons, with dispatches from Gibraltar and Lord Nelson."

Guns boom in salute to a squadron of 6 ships flying the flag of a distinguished ally, Russia. These ships are sailing half round Europe, some 4,500 miles, to support a Russian army in Corfu.

Two ships have been hired as naval transports. "*Duchess of Bedford* and *Lord Eldon* (transports) armed ships have received on board 300 tons of vegetables; will take bullocks from Coast of Barbary, or wherever else they may be purchased, to Lord Nelson's fleet. They sail tomorrow."

As England has no censorship over newspapers, there can be no secrecy about war preparations.

DOVER, ENGLAND

Snargate Street, behind the harbour, has 50 taverns within its length. A door of one bursts open and 2 marines, a boatswain and 2 sailors with truncheons drag out a drunken man. He struggles and shouts as they move off down the street. By the harbour a dirty building with small windows displays a naval ensign outside. This is where the press-gangs first take their captures, until a boat can take them off to a warship.

Since the war began Britain has been refitting old ships and building new ones to bring fleets up to strength; and ships need men. Some volunteer, but not nearly enough. Merchant sailors, criminals, soldier deserters, anyone without money or influence, are pressed into the Navy. Press-gangs comb every large port and dockyard town in England.

The *Diligence* sloop of war has arrived today, to be used as a receiving ship for impressed men. On the ship they are furling sails. Suddenly a long-drawn cry sounds across the water and abrubtly ceases.

"On Monday . . . a black sailor, belonging to the *Diligence* . . . while employed in the rigging, one of the topgallant yards giving way, was precipitated to the deck and so dreadfully bruised that he expired the next morning." Many pressed men, whipped aloft before they have experience, fall and die.

WOOLWICH DOCKYARD, NEAR LONDON, ENGLAND

In a vast wooden cradle on the slipway stands the largest ship in the Royal Navy, the *Ocean*, 98 guns, 15 years in building. She is within 4 days of launching. Newspapers say she "appeared like a town". Her lower deck is 190 ft. long; she has room for 120 guns. "Her sides were painted yellow, with black streaks, and a white bottom." On Thursday next, Londoners by the thousand will make the trip to Woolwich to see her launching.

FOLKESTONE, ENGLAND

The *Desperate* gun brig comes into the waters of the Ness Road with a flotilla of captures behind her. One captured ship carries a valuable French cargo, originally bound for Germany.

During the war, exceptional service is often rewarded with a "cruize". This can be ordered to the Captain of a ship smaller than a full ship of the line, and leaves him free to hunt for French or neutral vessels carrying French cargoes. The value of any "prizes" he may take, or the proportion he is allowed to keep, is, for a naval captain, the quickest way to a fortune.

11 a.m.

LIVERPOOL, ENGLAND

A thriving city of 80,000 people and, after London, the busiest port in Britain. In 2 miles of docks, trading ships from all parts of the world. 28 vessels arrived from the West Indies alone in the last week.

At Mr. Bennett's yard, by Bold Street, buyers are gathering to bid for 130 logs of "choice Cuba Mahogany", to be auctioned at noon.

In King's Dock, the *St. Andrew*, 210 tons, is up for sale. She "sails fast, and is well adapted for the African and W. India Trade," says *Gore's General Advertiser*. In other words, a Slaver.

Liverpool is the English port for the Slavers. Several smallish vessels, 90 ft. long, lie loading in the docks. Guns from Birmingham, metal goods, woollen and cotton cloth are stowing in the holds. These will sell to African and Arab chiefs on the African West Coast in exchange for slaves. The ships then sail the Atlantic, sell their cargoes of 300 to 400 Negroes in North or South America or the West Indies, and bring back raw cotton, rum and sugar to Liverpool. In just two years' time slavery will be abolished in Britain, though slave ships will risk capture for years afterwards.

A very different ship, the *Investigator*, is unloading. The wooden crates swinging up from her hold carry thousands of plants, rocks and drawings, the result of four years' exploration on the unknown Australian coastlands under the naturalist Robert Brown.

BOOTLE COMMON, OUTSIDE LIVERPOOL, ENGLAND

Captain Carmichael and Major Edward Brookes, of the Royal Liverpool Fusiliers, are about to settle "an affair of honour", the polite name for a duel. The *Leeds Mercury* tells the story:

The two men pace away from each other, halt, turn, and take aim. The Captain fires and just misses. The Major fires, afterwards, deliberately into the air. The Captain is outraged, and demands to be shot at. The Major refuses. The argument becomes heated and the two men nearly come to blows. The Major explains "he had no grudge against Capt. Carmichael" who had challenged the duel under wrong information.

Quiet at last, the two shake hands!

HULL HARBOUR, ENGLAND

A fleet of merchantmen, bound for Tonningen on the Elbe, awaits a naval escort. Moored at the quays is a merchant fleet just in last Saturday from the Baltic.

CORK HARBOUR, IRELAND

A storeship has sailed from Kinsale, 15 miles away, to Lord Gardner's squadron at Cork.

Gardner is tired of asking for a store depot to be built near by on Haulbowline Island. Engineer's reports, many letters, have done nothing to stir the British Admiralty. Today he writes again, to the new First Lord, about ". . . the great inconvenience which arises from the . . . naval stores being kept at Kinsale, a distance of five leagues. . . . The delay, expense and difficulty of getting the stores round to this harbour . . . is very great; with easterly and southerly winds is very frequently impossible."

ADMIRALTY, LONDON, ENGLAND

The nerve centre of the Navy, and therefore of the defence of Britain. Alone in a high room sits a man of 79; Lord Barham, First Lord of the Admiralty. He is reading reports, making notes in the margin. In his veined hands lie the fortunes of all squadrons on active service.

He was called to take charge on 30 April in the midst of crisis, the day when news reached London of Villeneuve's escape into the Atlantic. He found everything near chaos. "The Admiralty as well as myself are alarmed at the want of ships," he wrote. Few ships are building, also "the almost total want of oak timber in the dockyards" is serious.

Seamen are scarcer than ships. "Disgraces must follow the want of men. . . . At present we are in the utmost want of 6 to 7,000 men for immediate service, and no one prospect of having them," Barham writes to William Pitt, the Prime Minister. "Something must be done, and that soon. . . . If the fleet is not kept in motion and made adequate to our growing demands, we must sink under the preparations that are making against us."

On 1 August he suggests: "The State requiring that the king's ships now remaining in port . . . should be manned without the least delay, it is proposed . . . to ship owners . . . that one man in six will be taken from all ships and vessels howsoever protected . . ." Things are desperate. "We must therefore have resort to landsmen and the army in being employed afloat . . ." he writes two days later.

Barham reorganizes the Admiralty, finds somehow ships and men, chases supplies, above all directs the war at sea. All secret orders are signed by him. He sleeps at the Admiralty. "I seldom have the pen out of my hand from 8 in the morning till 6 at night."

In an age of bribery he is stern and fair to everyone. He writes to the King, excusing himself from attending court. Nelson, when he returned to England in August, had to send his ship's journal to Barham, so that the First Lord could judge this national hero for himself. Only after approving Nelson's reports did he give him command of the present Mediterranean fleet.

. . . Barham reads on, in silence. At every crisis since Villeneuve escaped, his orders, day after day, have

placed British squadrons in the point of need. He has outplayed Napoleon.

The last result of his tireless reorganization is a new set of Navy Regulations for January, 1806. One month after that, on the death of Pitt, a new government will retire him with little thanks. He will live on, unremembered, to the age of 87.

ADMIRALTY SECRETARY'S OFFICES

Today is a routine one for the Admiralty. No secret orders, no sudden information. In one of the clerks' rooms a quill slowly scratches a copy of the third out-letter of the day. It is to Nelson; it contains the last words written to him by anyone during his lifetime:

By Hand

Having ordered the Captain of H.M. Ship *Chiffone* to proceed with the two hired armed ships named in the margin—*Duchess of Bedford* and *Lord Eldon*—(which are to be employed for the purpose of procuring cattle and refreshments for the squadron under your Lordship's command) and use his best endeavours to join you, your Lordship is hereby required and directed to take him and the said Ships under your command accordingly.

Given the 21st October 1805
P. Patton
E. Nepean
Garlies.

The previous letter gives the necessary orders to Capt. Campbell of the *Chiffone*, waiting at Spithead. The letters will go with the special messenger by the evening coach to Portsmouth.

11 a.m.

WINDSOR, ENGLAND

The chimes of church clocks striking the hour mingle with a roar of cheers. Crowds of people squeezed on narrow pavements stretch and push to get a better view. Handkerchiefs wave and here and there a parasol shines out gaily in the autumn sun. The flash of harness, the livery of coachmen, and womens' brilliant dresses mark the position of landaus and barouches standing at the side of the street. Amid renewed cheers the procession passes from view towards the Castle.

"Their Majesties and the Princesses arrived at Windsor castle at 11 a.m. from Kew, escorted by a party of Royal Horse Guards, to inspect works going on in the castle," reports *The Times*.

Three months earlier, the American traveller, Benjamin Silliman, saw the King: "A noble-looking old man, fleshy, yet not oppressively corpulent, and his countenance is so highly coloured . . ."

Everyone knows about his occasional mad fits, yet George III is a popular King—although not with the Prince of Wales: the loathing between father and son is mutual. In five years' time the old King will be finally incapable of proper decisions, and authority will pass to the Prince, acting as his father's Regent.

RAMSGATE, ENGLAND

53 minutes before high water.

"The last division of Hanoverian Legion embarked at Ramsgate. Remainder of stores, artillery, will embark on Tuesday." *The Times*

The South of England is alive with marching men. A force is gathering under the command of General George Don which will land in North Germany within a month. The advance party of the King's German legion, backed by 2 English brigades, already numbers 11,000. Prussia, Sweden and Denmark will act with them to capture Holland from the French. "Two Battalions of Guards, the 4th, 14th, 23rd Regiments of Infantry, 5 Companies of 95th Rifle Reg. . . ., 4 Car Brigades of Artillery all to embark. . . ." *The Times*

Some miles off-shore a group of transports ride at anchor. They are fishing-craft hired from private owners. "There are in the Downs several large boats, resembling a ship's launch, each mounting one carronade of large calibre, and capable of carrying 50 soldiers."

SANDWICH, ENGLAND

The Deal to Sandwich road is crowded with other troops, carts and horses bound for Ramsgate harbour.

The 1st Btn. of the 95th Regiment is dusty and tired. The men have tramped 15 miles since early morning, when they passed through Dover at 6. In fields outside the town they are due for a halt, with bread and cheese. Muskets are heavy, and fifes and drums are silent. The next day the *Kentish Gazette* describes the end of their march at 3 this afternoon:

"As soon as they arrived at our barracks, they were handsomely regaled with several butts of strong beer . . . after regaling themselves for about 2 hours, both battalions, amounting to more than 2,000, marched to the pier, and went immediately on board the transports, singing 'Rule Britannia' in high spirits, and this morning (Tuesday) the whole sailed for the Downs."

DEAL, ENGLAND

Specially built flat-bottomed boats are about to leave the beaches at high water. They also are bound for the troopships off Ramsgate.

DOVER, ENGLAND

Here, too, people stand and stare at troops. The 43rd and 52nd Regiments have just marched in to relieve the 3rd Coldstream Reg. of Guards. The Guards will leave on Wednesday to embark at Ramsgate.

NEWHAVEN, ENGLAND

The 2nd Btn. of the Enniskillen Regiment of Foot has marched in 400 miles from Edinburgh Castle also to join the expedition.

BRIGHTON, ENGLAND

The Welsh Somerset Militia has arrived from Weymouth en route for Silverhill Barracks. "Four soldiers broke in the store-room of Mr. Coates' White Lion public house" and one drank himself unconscious, being ill for days, says the *Brighton Weekly Advertiser*. As Silliman says: "The life of a common soldier is, in every part of it, deplorable. His pay is a song, his service is severe, his privations great, his dangers frequent . . . his death . . . unlamented, or, if he survives, his old age is dependent, vacant, and miserable."

HARWICH, ENGLAND

Britain is worried about the Austrians. "General Ramsay at Harwich to embark for continent to be with Austrian Armies, to send back news."

11.15 a.m.

THE POOL OF LONDON, ENGLAND

The wide reaches of the Thames below London Bridge form the busiest port in the world. The early fog has lifted, but above the forest of masts that line each side of the river, smoke and steam hang in a yellow haze. Gulls scream as they circle over the dirty water. Merchantmen flying flags of all nations are moored to wharves, and between them small boats are everywhere. "The innumerable wherries, passage boats, lighters and other small craft, swam on its surface, like insects on a pool of stagnant water, in a summer's morning," was how Silliman saw it a few months earlier, on his way to Holland.

At Rotherhythe on the South bank, thick black smoke and a poisonous smell marks the dock for Greenland whalers. Men in long leather jackets stoke the fires under great cauldrons where the blubber is boiling down for oil.

Opposite on the North bank the New London docks were opened in May; the East and West India docks three years before in 1802. Cottons from India, tea, sugar, spices from the East, flow into the Port of London. Many ships bring live animals. *The Times* today advertises:

TURTLES. *Richard's Coffee House, Covent Garden, just arrived from W. Indies, a few fine lively turtles, and also dresses this day a remarkably fine one, with greatest culinary attention. Any quantity packed in jars, and warranted good, to all parts of England.*

Barrels swing in the air; ropes creak on wooden pulleys. This year more and more steam-engines ponderously crank round their heavy fly-wheels to wind cranes.

Two steam-locomotives, built by Richard Tevithick, the Cornish inventor, proved too heavy for their rails; but his stationary engines, now set up throughout England and Wales, pump water and drive winding-gear of all kinds. Last year alone, at least 50 were built.

At Customs House some travellers stand with their baggage. They are in a hurry to catch the packet for Harwich, sailing in three hours with the tide. Seasoned travellers know that a bribe is needed to save days of delay in clearing their luggage. A half-crown slipped in the official's hand, and he opens the bags, puts in a finger, says everything is in order without a second glance, and the job is done. The upright Silliman objected strongly, but he had to pay up.

GREENFORD GREEN, ENGLAND

The 8 a.m. daily packet from Paddington is exactly half-way to Uxbridge, by the Grand Union Canal. It will arrive at 3 p.m. doing the $17\frac{1}{2}$ miles in 7 hours. It will set off back again from Uxbridge at 4, bringing at least some sacks of the fine white flour which Uxbridge windmills are famous for.

The great age of canal building began with the Worsley Canal built by James Brindley 33 years before, for the Duke of Bridgewater. By now there are canals all over England; they provide the cheapest transport for goods. At the steady, measured pace of the powerful shire-horses which tow the barges, independent of snow and mud which clog the roads in winter, the bulk of merchandise between cities now goes by water. To keep their level, canals pass over roads by viaducts, and tunnel through hills, changing level when needed by means of locks.

11.30 a.m.

VALETTA HARBOUR, MALTA

40 troopships, that sailed from England last April, lie anchored on the still water. 6 battalions of infantry are waiting for dinner. Some detachments are allowed on shore, but most men are sleeping, washing, or card-playing on mess decks. After a chequered voyage, this expedition, under General Sir James Craig, reached here on 18 July. In 9 days' time the General will be ordered to take his troops to meet the Russians at Syracuse and sail with them to defend Naples.

MESSINA, SICILY

A cloudless sky, with the sun nearly at its zenith. From the shade of a fig-tree a young English poet overlooks the Straits between Sicily and the Italian mainland. He carries a canvas satchel and a notebook. He is on holiday, with time to stare, and the world seems new.

He came from England as under-secretary to the British Government at Malta. At this time a skill in Latin, good manners, and a few influential friends are enough to start one on a career as a diplomat. He wrote reports in a dusty office from May 1804 to last September, but now he has had enough of it. He is on his way home.

His name, Samuel Taylor Coleridge, is known already for the poem, "The Ancient Mariner". Today is his thirty-third birthday. Yesterday he wrote in his notebook:

". . . and beyond it I see the open Sea, which by the hither Shore and the Coast of Calabria appears shaped as a wedge with an indefinite Base/ the Ships, the beautiful Sparonaras, the fishing Boats, the white Sails of the Mediterranean."

Taking his time, meandering by by-ways and detours, he will arrive at Naples on 15 December; and finally, penniless and exhausted, at Kent in England in August one year later.

It is here, at Messina, in just four months' time, that the King and Queen of Naples will take refuge from the victorious French invaders.

HERCULANEUM, 7 MILES EAST OF NAPLES, ITALY

Mr. Hayter and 11 students are walking along a tunnel below ground. Their morning's work is finished.

Buried centuries ago by black lava from Vesuvius, the ancient Roman city has been dug into and its bronze statues lifted for many years past.

Hayter has come from England to examine the library of scrolls buried in the Villa Suburbana. The fragile scrolls—the earliest form of books—are sliced into sections and copied piece by piece. Mostly they are works of Epicurean philosophy. A report of their work, sent by Baron Kotzebue, has just reached England. The person paying expenses is—the Prince of Wales.

NAPLES, THE PALAZZO STESSA, ITALY

The British Embassy. In a magnificent room, Hugh Elliot, the British Ambassador, finishes the morning's letters. It is now over 12 years since the wife of another ambassador, in this palace, first set eyes on the young English captain of the *Agamemnon*. The ambassador was Sir William Hamilton; his wife the young and beautiful Emma; the captain—plain Horatio Nelson. Nelson then little thought that she would become the idol of his life. He wrote to his wife at the time: "Lady Hamilton has been wonderfully kind and good to Josiah [Nelson's stepson]. She is a young woman of amiable manners, and who does honour to the station to which she is raised." Careful words for the beginning of such a story!

BAY OF NAPLES, ITALY

The *Excellent*, British ship of the line, lies at anchor. Sent by Nelson, it has waited many months now for the day when the Bourbon King and Queen of Naples, enemies to Napoleon, will need a safe passage to exile in Sicily. It is for Naples that Gravina and Villeneuve are bound with the combined fleets, on Napoleon's orders. They are intending to capture the *Excellent* and land 4,000 French troops in the Bay, to link up with the French army to the east.

On board the *Excellent*, a letter from Nelson lies on Captain Sotheron's table. It is the last message that Sotheron will ever have from his commander. Only two days after joining the British fleet off Cadiz, and amidst a spate of official instructions and orders, Nelson found time to write this personal note:

Victory, September 30th, 1805.
My dear Sotheron,

Captain Tyler's son is adrift in Italy, at Naples, or Rome; we think, very probably, in prison for debt. His father is very anxious to save the lad. He was Lieutenant of the *Hydra* and ran away with an opera-dancer from Malta. Pray try . . . to get word of Mr. Tyler. Captain Tyler will pay the bills he has drawn for on England—supposed to be two or three hundred pounds—and if now a few more is necessary to liberate the youth, I will be answerable. All we want is to save him from perdition . . .

Ever . . . your much obliged friend,
NELSON AND BRONTE

Nelson's diagram in his Memorandum.

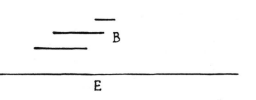

Method of Attack probably planned by Nelson

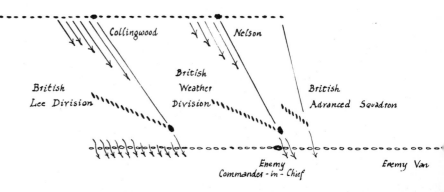

Position of Fleets in Actual Battle at 11.45 a.m.

British ➤

Weather Division

1 Victory (Nelson)
2 Téméraire
3 Neptune
4 Leviathan
5 Conqueror
6 Agamemnon
7 Britànnia
8 Ajax
9 Orion
10 Minotaur
11 Spartiate
12 Africa

Lee Division

13 Royal Sovereign
  (Collingwood)
14 Belleisle
15 Mars
16 Collossus
17 Tonnant
18 Bellerophon
19 Achille
20 Polyphemus
21 Revenge
22 Swiftsure
23 Defence
24 Thunderer
25 Prince
26 Defiance
27 Dreadnought

Allied ⊶

French ⊸

2 Scipion
4 Formidable
  (Dumanoir)
5 Mont Blanc
7 Duguay Trouin
9 Heros
12 Bucentaure
  (Villeneuve)
13 Neptune
14 Redoutable
16 Indomptable
18 Fougueux
20 Pluton
21 Intrépide
23 L'Aigle
25 Swiftsure
27 Argonaute
29 Achille
30 Algeçiras
33 Berwick

Spanish ⊶

1 Neptuno
3 S. Augustino
6 Rayo
8 Asis
10 S. Trinidada (Cisnera...
11 S. Justo
15 S. Leandro
17 St. Ana (D'Alica)
19 Monatca
22 Montanez
24 Asturias (Gravina)
26 Bahama
28 Ildefonso
31 Argonauta
32 S. Juan

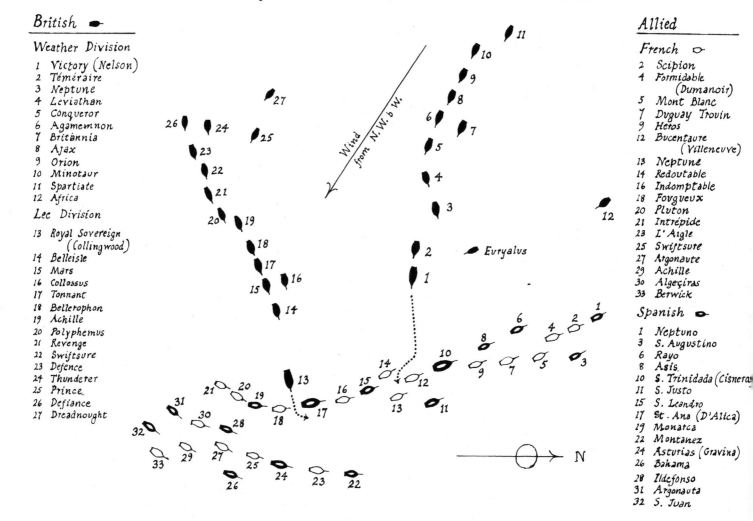

Allied ships cover British by their field of fire during whole time of British advance, once British are within gun range

British field of fire covers enemy ships only when Allied line is actually broken

11.45 a.m.

AT SEA, OFF CAPE TRAFALGAR

Fleets 1½ miles apart.

The British number 27 battleships of the line, plus 4 frigates, 1 schooner and 1 cutter. The French and Spanish have 33 of the line, plus 5 frigates and 2 brigs. The British are sailing now in 2 lines of battle: the lee division led by Collingwood in the *Royal Sovereign*; the weather division, to windward, led by Nelson in the *Victory*. This is the largest ship in the British fleet, 227 ft. long, 100 guns, plus carronades.

Ships of the line have 2 or 3 gun-decks; the Spanish flagship, the huge *Santissima Trinidada*, 130 guns, is a 4-decker. The heaviest guns are on the lower decks.

A fleet's order of sailing is in line ahead, the Admiral's flagship leading. Usual order of battle is in one or more lines, with the Admiral at the centre. The Admiral commanding a fleet can hoist his flag in any ship, even a frigate, but usually hides from the enemy until the last moment. When smoke blots out the Admiral's signals during battle, frigates must repeat them to distant ships.

Guns usually fire solid shot, from 6 to 32 lb. in weight, to a maximum range of 1½ miles. A heavy ball will burst through 3 ft. of timber at 500 yards. Gunfire can be aimed at masts and rigging to disable an enemy (the French practice); at the hull to kill men and smash guns (the British practice). Marines can fire muskets on enemy deck-officers; a ship can be hooked with grappling-irons and then boarded; it may be holed in so many places below the water-line as to sink; it can catch fire; or explode if its magazine is hit. Guns are muzzle-loading with powder bags, wadding and shot. They fire, with little traverse to left or right, through ports in the ship's sides. When possible, a ship is steered so that all guns on one side are fired together in broadside. In effect, ships can only fire on an enemy lying on either beam.

The fastest gun-teams at Trafalgar are on Collingwood's *Royal Sovereign*. The "Tars of the Tyne" come, like Collingwood, from Newcastle, or from Shields. Trained by daily practice on his last ship *Dreadnought*, they can get off 3 broadsides in 90 seconds.

Nelson's problem is (1) to destroy or capture the enemy fleet before it can escape back to Cadiz while (2) keeping himself clear of the shoals of Trafalgar which lie behind. An attacking fleet will normally sail so that, when in gun-range, it can turn in line, allowing all ships to fire broadsides at once. In the eighteenth century fleets often sailed in opposite directions but parallel, firing as they passed.

But Nelson is set on a real decision by all-out battle. Months ago, when he was on leave in England, a general plan of attack took shape in his mind. He said then: "No day can be long enough to arrange a couple of fleets and fight a decisive battle according to the old system. . . . I shall go at them at once, if I can, about one third of their line from their leading ship. . . . I think it will surprise and confound the enemy. They won't know what I am about. It will bring on a pell-mell battle, and that is what I want."

On 9 October, he wrote the details in a memorandum. To be ready for instant attack, the fleet's order of sailing will be also the order of battle, in 2 divisions of 16 ships each, heaviest gun-ships leading. The 2 flagships, Nelson's and Collingwood's, will be second and third in their respective divisions. 8 fast ships will be in reserve.

Collingwood will begin the attack by cutting off the rearmost 12 of the enemy line. His 16 ships will, each in turn, cut between each pair of the enemy. Meanwhile Nelson will direct his line just forward of the enemy centre in order to cut off the Commander-in-Chief. No details are laid down for Nelson's line, except that its main job is to leave Collingwood free to "effectually complete the business of twelve sail of the enemy." By the time the enemy van can wear and sail back to help the rest, the greater part of their fleet should be destroyed.

Now he is 13 ships short (5 on escort with Rear-Admiral Louis, one carrying Calder back to a court-martial, 7 not arrived from England). Doing away with a reserve, he has placed all ships in 2 divisions, 15 under Collingwood, 12 with himself.

In today's battle there are other changes from the plan. The 2 flagships are actually leading their divisions, at full speed and with every sail set. Rearmost ships have no chance to close up in normal battle line-abreast; some are straggling far behind. Never before has a line-ahead broken a properly formed fleet. In theory it is the weakest of all attacks, leaving each ship in turn a prey to massed gun-fire. Coming in at right-angles to the enemy line, the British risk being shot to pieces before they can bring a single gun to bear in reply.

But for the first time on record a major attack is developing under full sail instead of reduced fighting-sails, and for the first time all the heaviest fire-power is in the lead. Nelson has staked everything on surprise, on speed, on the gamble that the wind will not die completely, and on heavier gun-power at the point of impact.

11.50 a.m.

AT SEA, OFF CAPE TRAFALGAR

Sky overcast. Wind dying to lightest breezes.

The French and Spanish fleet is waiting, motionless, heads to the wind, in one curving line, with many ships doubled behind each other. Allied officers are puzzled, even amazed. There is still no sign of check in the leading British ships, no deployment for battle. A kind of attack no one has dreamed of is taking place before their eyes. By all laws it is madness. Nelson will surely be destroyed.

Ahead of the whole British fleet, alone, silent, sailing without a pause into the midst of the massed Allied line, is the *Royal Sovereign*. It is an uncanny, to some an unnerving sight.

Villeneuve watches the British divisions advancing. They seem to be aiming for his centre and rear. Since reversing his line by wearing, Gravina's observation squadron is now in the rear; but for some reason the Spanish Admiral has not kept out to windward from where he could sail to any threatened area. The old rear, under Vice-Admiral Dumanoir, is now the van. Villeneuve still cannot be sure just where Nelson will strike. All he can do is wait. General signal 242 "Open fire" flies from the *Bucentaure*, meaning his ships are to fire when in range.

From the *Victory*, Badcock watches the enemy. "It was a beautiful sight when their line was completed: their broadsides turned towards us showing their iron teeth . . .

"In our fleet Union Jacks and ensigns were made fast to the fore and fore-topmast-stays, as well as to the mizen rigging, besides one at the peak, in order that we might not mistake each other in the smoke . . ." In addition, Nelson has ordered the iron mast-hoops on all British ships to be whitewashed so that, should flags be shot away, the British can still be distinguished from the enemy, whose hoops are black.

In the last moments before battle, Nelson's nerves are stretched almost to breaking. Pacing the poop with his frigate captains and Captain Hardy, he decides to make a signal message to the fleet: "Nelson confides that every man will do his duty." Blackwood and Hardy suggest that the word "England" would be better than "Nelson". The admiral at once agrees.

Flag-Lieutenant Pasco is in charge of signals on the *Victory*. He says: "His Lordship came to me on the poop, and . . . said: 'Mr Pasco, I want to say to the fleet, "England confides that every man will do his duty."' He added, 'You must be quick, for I have one more to add, which is for "Close Action!"'" Pasco reads numbers from Sir Home Popham's new signal code, issued 6 weeks before to battle squadrons. He reports that "confides" would need spelling, letter by letter, whereas "expects" is in the code. Nelson hastily agrees to the second change. "That will do, Pasco; make it directly."

Signalman John Roome, a young Thames bargehand press-ganged into the *Victory* two years before, begins tying the flags. Pasco says: "As the last hoist was hauled down, Nelson turned to Captain Blackwood . . . with, 'Now I can do no more. We must trust to the great Disposer of all events . . .' When Lord Nelson's message had been answered . . . he ordered me to make the signal for 'Close Action' and keep it up. Accordingly I hoisted No. 16 at the top-gallant masthead, and there it remained until shot away."

The *Royal Sovereign*, every sail fully set, nearly a mile ahead of the rest of the fleet, is almost within range of enemy guns. Collingwood, round faced, calm, eats an apple as he walks the quarter-deck. Gunners lie flat on their stomachs, waiting.

The signal lieutenant begins writing numbers on his slate. The *Victory* is telegraphing the fleet: 253, 269, 863, 261, 471, 958, 220, 370, 4, 21, 19, 24. Collingwood is in no mood for further messages. "I wish Nelson would stop signalling," he grumbles. "We all know what we have to do." The numbers are deciphered from the code book, and the signal read out:

"England expects that every man will do his DUTY."

Frigates repeat it, it is noted in ships' logs, on some ships it is read to the men. Some are puzzled; then volleys of cheering sound across the water.

Noon

LONDON, ENGLAND

"No, Sir, when a man is tired of London he is tired of life;" said Samuel Johnson 28 years before.

From Piccadilly to Houndsditch a medley of pleasure and business, of riches and poverty. Everywhere shouts and cries, the stench of horse-dung, the grate of iron-tipped wheels on cobbles, the bells of Wren's city churches tolling the hour. St. Paul's towers high over all, its dome a landmark that can be seen from as far as the fields of Hampstead.

In the streets rogues of all kinds. dealing in smuggled goods. A short. fat man in a scarlet waistcoat is the one Silliman met. "'Young gentleman, Sir, your honour!' So many titles made me stop, when he put his mouth to my ear, and said in a low voice: 'I've got some nice French Cambric—will you buy?'"

Londoners have many prejudices, but seldom against colour. As Silliman noticed: "A black footman is considered a great acquisition . . . Negro servants are sought after and caressed. An ill-dressed or starving Negro is never seen in England. A few days ago I met in Oxford Street a well-dressed white girl . . . walking arm in arm with a Negro man, who was as well dressed as she."

Lloyds, in the Royal Exchange, is crowded and excited. The news of the safe arrival of the West Indian fleets is just out. Insurers feel a weight off their shoulders and are in a gay mood. The capture of a merchant fleet by the French, or pirates, could spell ruin to some underwriters.

STANHOPE STREET, LONDON

The Countess Conyngham gives birth to a son. Possibly her lady's maid will show her an advertisement in today's *Times*:
WANTED, *by a young woman, with a good breast of milk, 5 miles from town, a child to wet-nurse; she has no young of her own, and can be well recommended. Reply to E.T. at Mr. Chatline's, Grocer, Wandsworth, Surrey.*

Well-to-do mothers seldom feed their own babies.

There are other animals than horses and dogs. Silliman again, writing in the summer of this year: "I had almost reached my lodgings, when I was saluted by martial music. which I thought must proceed from a regiment of volunteers . . . but, on turning the corner of Margaret Street, what should I see but a camel, directly before my windows. The music preceded the camel, which was led by a man, while a monkey, dressed in a scarlet military coat . . . was mounted on the back. . . . To increase the mirth, a boy mounted the camel, and the little red coated equestrian took his station on the boy's head. . . . The camel seemed rather dispirited and poor in flesh; he was reluctant to move, as the rough stones of the pavement appeared to hurt his feet . . . he would not stir without whipping, and then uttered a piteous noise like a groan."

People of every kind. On the one hand, knock-knees, hunched shoulders, the twisted foot and stunted growth from underfeeding. On the other, from gross overeating, the gout. Silliman: "As I was walking along the Strand, I accidentally trod on the toes of a true John Bull, who was hobbling along on his cane . . . I begged his pardon. . . . 'Beg Pardon!' cried he . . . he corrugated his features most hideously, and raising his cane . . . he poured forth such a flood of execrations, till they died away in the hum of the crowd."

Everywhere beggars. A regular colony lives at Seven Dials in Soho, and children with broken limbs are sent to beg for their families. "There is an unfortunate man . . . in Holborn . . . he has neither legs nor thighs. He sits upon a little sled, to which he is fastened by straps, and moves himself by crutches, raising the sled with himself at every effort. He never begs. He merely sits upon his sled, with his hat in his hand. . . . Such has been his success that (as report says) he has given a daughter in marriage with a portion of several hundred pounds."

Ex-soldiers too. "At present, considerable numbers of soldiers who lost their eyes in the Egyptian expedition are begging their bread in the streets of London. This misfortune befell multitudes of them in the burning deserts of Egypt and Syria, from the heat and the sand."

For stall-holders, life is tough. Silliman writes: "I was, yesterday, passing through a narrow lane, leading into Oxford Road, when I saw a very athletic woman dragging by the collar a man much stouter than herself, and, with very appropriate eloquence, upbraiding him for attempting to go off without paying for some cherries . . . greatly to the diversion of the populace, as she brought him back to her wheelbarrow."

For the tourist, there are lions, a tiger, a polar bear, leopards, panthers, wolves, hyenas, racoons to be seen in a den at the Tower. Brook's animal shop, at the corner of Piccadilly and Haymarket, has a llama for sale. It disliked Silliman, spraying him with "a greenish fluid". But many gentlemen keep wild animals as pets.

Noon

Captured after fierce fighting in torrential rain, 7 days before. Napoleon sits writing to his wife at Strasbourg: Oct. 21.

I am fairly well, my dear. I start at once for Augsbourg. I have made 33,000 men lay down their arms, I have from 60,000 to 70,000 prisoners, more than 90 flags, and 200 pieces of cannon. Never has there been such a catastrophe in military annals. Take care of yourself. I am rather jaded. The weather has been fine for the last 3 days. The first column of prisoners files off for France today. Each column consists of 6,000 men.

NAPOLEON.

He is neatly, though soberly, dressed. At 36, he is beginning to put on weight. His imposing head is large for his height—5 ft. 2 in. His hands and feet are small.

He loves France, yet distrusts her people. "What they need is glory, the satisfactions of vanity," he once said. He is Emperor, with absolute power. His secretary, Baron de Méneval, wrote much about him: "When he was excited . . . his face became stern and even terrible. . . . His eyes hurled lightning. The wings of his nose dilated . . . Napoleon rarely wrote himself . . . his writing was a collection of letters unconnected with each other, and unreadable." His brain stores vast quantities of facts, yet can work with incredible speed. "Napoleon used to explain . . . that the various subjects were arranged in his head, as though in a cupboard. 'When I want to interrupt one piece of work,' he used to say, 'I close the drawer in which it is, and I open another . . . when I want to go to sleep, I close up all the drawers . . .'"

Louis Bourrienne, Napoleon's early friend, said: "Bonaparte had some curious habits. Whenever he was crossed or absorbed in some unpleasant idea, he used to hum what was not a tune or anything like one, his voice . . . being so unmusical. He would sit at his desk, and then tilt his chair till I frequently had to warn him he might fall over backwards . . . he would vent his ill-humour on the right arm of the chair, mutilating it with his penknife . . ."

One campaign is over; another is about to begin. "The weather is frightful," he had written on the 12th, and two days ago: "Soaked clothes and cold feet every day for a week." All morning he has been reading reports, dictating orders. The corridors have echoed to the boots of generals, adjutants, secretaries. "He would rise slowly, and begin to walk slowly up and down the whole length of the room . . . inspiration . . . showed itself by a nervous trick which he had of twisting his right arm whilst pulling at the trimmings of his sleeve with his hand . . ." said Méneval.

In another room secretaries copy the bulletin he has dictated today.

9th Bulletin de la Grande Armée. 21 October.

"Here is the number of our prisoners," it announces. "10,000 in Augsbourg; 33,000 in Ulm; 12,000 at Donauwœrth, and 12,000 already en route for France. . . . In the French army, the highest heroism; in the Austrian, the depths of despair . . ."

Yesterday, from 2 in the afternoon until 7 in the evening, Napoleon stood on a hill-side 1 mile north of Ulm, while 33,000 Austrian soldiers filed past and laid down their arms.

In the court-yard stand the palace sentries. Wherever Napoleon has his camp, on campaign, the place is called the "Palace". The sentries are from the Imperial Guard. This is the élite of the army. Each year one man is chosen from each line battalion, 2 from each cavalry and artillery regiment, to have the honour of joining the Guard. The Guard sets a standard for other regiments to look up to. It provides the Emperor's personal bodyguard of one infantry battalion and one cavalry squadron which always surrounds him. Its soldiers get special pay. It forms the final reserve of the army, only used in special need.

More than 10,000 strong, it includes regiments of foot Grenadiers, horse Grenadiers (all huge men), Chasseurs (light horse), Chasseurs à Cheval (guides), Vélites (young cadets), Marines, and Mamelukes. The Mamelukes are native horsemen from Egypt, descended from white Turkish slaves. Each company is led by French officers.

They are fierce fighters, magnificent horsemen, and superbly dressed in Eastern costume. Imitations of their turbans and Turkish trousers are all the rage in Paris. Many French officers, even infantrymen, carry scimitars like theirs. Roustam, Napoleon's personal and devoted slave, is a Mameluke.

Outside one can hear shouts, orders, the jingle of harness and the clatter of horses on the cobbles.

Napoleon's coach is waiting.

Noon

MERTON, ENGLAND

Through the bedroom windows of Merton House a view of lawns, shrubberies, and just the top of a vine-covered verandah. Emma, Lady Hamilton, 42 years old, widow of the elderly ambassador to Naples, mistress to Nelson, is in bed. Still strikingly good-looking, though heavy now and with a coarsened skin, she is propped on a mass of pillows.

With company, no one is more conscious of Nelson's honour than Emma. Sir Gilbert Elliot wrote before Trafalgar: "She goes on cramming Nelson with trowelfulls of flattery, which he goes on taking as quietly as a child does pap. Not only the rooms but the whole house, staircase and all, are covered with nothing but pictures of him and her, of all sizes and sorts, and representations of his naval actions, coats of arms, pieces of plate in his honour, the flagstaff of *L'Orient*, etc." Now the house seems empty after the parties and guests of Nelson's last stay. A breakfast tray is by her bed.

She glances idly at the October issue of *The Lady's Monthly Museum*. It carries part of a long serial, "The Romance of her Pyrenees". She reads fitfully: her own life, from country servant-girl to bosom friend of the Queen of Naples, makes perhaps a greater adventure than those in books.

CAMBRIDGE, ENGLAND

A young man on horseback emerges from the shadow of Queen's Gate into Trinity Lane. He is expensively though oddly dressed in a flowing silver-grey coat and white hat; his grey horse is beautifully groomed. He is an undergraduate more concerned with his horse than his studies, and more with his £500 yearly allowance than either. He is 17, handsome, clever, and determined to follow the fashion in doing as little work as possible. This is his second day at Cambridge; his first letter, 5 days later, will be to his lawyer:

From Trinity College.
          October 26 1805.
To John Hansom:
   Dear Sir, I will be obliged to you to order me down 4 Dozen of Wine, Port, Sherry, Claret, and Madeira, one dozen of each. I have got part of my furniture in, and begin to admire a College life. Yesterday my appearance in the Hall in my State Robes was Superb, but uncomfortable. . . . You may order the Saddle, etc, etc, for 'Oateater' as soon as you please . . .
   I remain, Sir, Yours truly,
            BYRON.

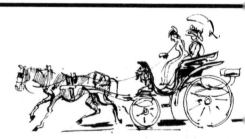

HYDE PARK, LONDON, ENGLAND

The cockneys who strolled here yesterday in holiday get-up are all back at work. On an Autumn weekday, there are more carriages than walkers. Rich young ladies have discovered the pleasures of exercise. A soft thud of hooves, a cloud of dust, and the two young ladies Silliman saw in September pass by in their phaeton. Following, at a discreet distance, are two watchful footmen. "Driving is quite fashionable among ladies of England," Silliman notes, "our female charioteer had the very equestrian air; . . . and she cracked the whip, and humoured the reins so well, that one would think she had been taking lessons from a master."

32, SOHO SQUARE, LONDON

Sir Joseph Banks, President of the Royal Society, is entertaining in his library. A great botanist and explorer, he has studied plants in Newfoundland, the Hebrides and Iceland. Thirty-five years ago he sailed round the world with Captain James Cook. He is the organizer of most British exploration of the time: to the Arctic, to Africa, to Australia, to Syria. Now he leans heavily on a stick, and looks older than his 61 years.

Scientists like James Watt, the inventor of the steam-engine, philosophers, and explorers gather at his house daily. "They constitute his court, and they would not dishonour the King himself," thought Silliman. "There was no ceremony of any kind. They came, and departed when they pleased." It is open house from 10 a.m. breakfast to 4 in the afternoon. The librarian of all the huge collection of books is Swedish and many of the visitors are foreigners.

ALBANY HOUSE, PICCADILLY, LONDON, ENGLAND

Since early morning, 3 children have died in London from smallpox. During the 3 weeks ending 14 October, one died, on average, every 2 hours. Most people agree that inoculation has proved a protection against the terrible disease, but Britain is about the last country in Europe to adopt the idea.

Dr. Moseley, eminent and rich, is today writing another strong letter to the *Gentleman's Magazine* against the new-fangled and "filthy practice" of inoculation.

GATEATON STREET, LONDON

Dr. Mendoza eyes his afternoon's assortment of patients. His Monday surgery, from 12 to 3, has just begun. Bleeding is still a common remedy for many ailments. No one knows much about germs, and things are none too clean . . .

NEW BOOKS ON SALE TODAY

'Fables, Ancient and Modern' for children, 73 engravings, price 8/-.

Dr. Thornton's *'Temple of Flora'*, with 30 hand-coloured engravings of plants, and poetry, price 25/-.

For politically-minded readers, the *'War in Disguise, or the fraud of the neutral flags'* at Hatchard's in Piccadilly.

FLEET STREET, LONDON, ENGLAND

Laurie and Whittle's print-shop has a new print today in the window: "Taking an airing at Brighton, the Donkies, or the Humours of Fashion", by Isaac Cruikshank. At Ackermann's shop in the Strand, they are still showing a print by the great Rowlandson: "Departure from Coast, or the end of the Farce of Invasion." Prints are enormously popular and can be enjoyed even by people who can't read. If one can't afford to buy, one can always hire a book of them by the evening, and if one is too poor for that there is always the window to stare at free.

GARRAWAY'S AUCTION ROOMS, LONDON, ENGLAND

"Going to the gentleman on my left!" A large crowd of land speculators watches the bids closely. 400 acres of meadowland at Farringdon, and 2,000 feet of open land at Windmill Lane, Camberwell (suitable to build small houses on), are the 2 main items of the day. Population is booming: two years ago it had reached 838,000; everywhere houses are building, eating farther into London's fields.

68, LOWER GROSVENOR STREET, LONDON, ENGLAND

There is always magic in strange lands. Here a Frenchman, Du Bourg, exhibits a working model of the volcano Vesuvius. Admission costs 2/-. Silliman thought the show well worth it. "Behind a curtain where all was dark, we perceived Mount Vesuvius throwing out fire, red-hot stones, smoke and flame, with a roaring noise like thunder; the crater glowed with heat, and . . . the lava . . . poured down a torrent of liquid fire. . . . The waves of the sea are in motion . . . the flames, cinders, fiery stones, etc., are all real. . . . Du Bourg has not forgotten to appeal to the sense of smell . . . for the spectator is assailed by the odour of burning sulphur."

Noon

The *Royal Sovereign* enters the fire zone. A sudden burst of yellow flame, dissolving to heavy smoke, comes from the French *Fougueux*. Cannon-balls whine by and splash in the sea.

As if by signal all admirals, French, Spanish, British, hoist their flags. Each Spanish ship hangs a large wooden cross from the end of its spanker boom. On French ships, drums play and soldiers present arms. Villeneuve signals: "Every ship which is not in action is not at its post . . ."

The *Royal Sovereign* closes towards the *Santa Ana*, 112 guns, flying the flag of the Spanish Vice-Admiral de Alava. The British ship comes under fire from all sides. The *Fougueux*, 74 guns, draws in close behind the *Santa Ana*. "Steer straight for the Frenchman and take his bowsprit," Collingwood orders.

12.10 p.m.

Through dense smoke Collingwood's gunners at last see from their gun-ports the stern of the *Santa Ana*, at point blank range. They fire a 50 gun broadside, guns double-shotted, straight into the Spanish hull. Over 200 Spaniards are killed or wounded and 14 guns

disabled. Broadsides answer each other in a continual thunder; the ships can scarcely be seen for the pall of smoke hanging in the still air.

12.20 p.m.

2 miles north-west. The *Victory* is $1\frac{1}{4}$ miles from the allied line, sailing silently. Wind almost dead; her speed down to $1\frac{1}{2}$ m.p.h.

A ranging shot from the *Bucentaure* falls short.

Victory, to fleet, signals No. 16 "Engage enemy more closely".

Two minutes later a second shot splashes alongside. A third drones over the masts. Finally the main top-gallant sail is holed. Again silence.

Nelson decides to cut through the enemy line at the 13th or 14th ship from the front, then attack the van from leeward. He sends off his frigate captains to tell the other ships.

12.30 p.m.

Victory one mile from enemy. The silence is broken. 8 allied ships open up together with full broadsides. Wind only a breath, but her earlier impetus drives the

44

Victory forward. The murderous fire begins to tell. Nelson's secretary, Mr. Scott, is killed. One double-headed shot kills 8 marines on the poop. The deck wheel is smashed; steering is now by ropes in the gun-room. A shot crashes between Nelson and Hardy on the quarter-deck, striking up a splinter which tears off Hardy's shoe-buckle. "This is too warm work, Hardy, to last long," is Nelson's comment. At 500 yards the mizen topmast is shot away. Sails are torn to rags; every studding sail boom is shot off.

At last Nelson sees Villeneuve's flag, on the *Bucentaure*. At all costs the Commander-in-Chief must be cut off. Nelson steers for a gap between the *Bucentaure* and the *Trinidada*. Villeneuve closes up and Nelson has to steer astern. This gap too is filled, by the French *Redoutable*. Hardy tells him the *Victory* won't get through. Nelson replies: "I cannot help it. . . . Go on board which you please: take your choice."

12.55 p.m.

William Willmet, the *Victory*'s bos'n, fires the 68 lb. forecastle carronade, with one round shot and 500 musket-balls, into the *Bucentaure*'s cabin windows.

Moving slowly past, each of the 50 port guns in turn, double and treble-shotted, tears into the *Bucentaure*'s stern. Nearly half the French crew are killed or wounded. Deck officers on the *Victory* are smothered in white dust from the smashed woodwork. On the gun-decks below, men choke in the dense black smoke pouring back inboard.

With helm hard to port the *Victory* crashes in on the side of the *Redoutable*. The ships lock together with entangled spars and fire at point-blank range. Lucas's men from the rigging of the *Redoutable* sweep the *Victory* with muskets and grenades.

1.15 p.m.

Amid gun-smoke, dust and musket-fire Nelson paces the quarter-deck amidships, with Hardy. He is turning about; then, suddenly, he falls on his knees and left hand. He collapses on his left side, on the same spot where Scott was killed, among Scott's bloodstains. Captain Hardy and a marine sergeant and two sailors lift him. Nelson speaks in gasps: "They have done for me at last, Hardy . . . my backbone is shot through."

1.20 p.m.

HOUNSLOW, ENGLAND

"A pitched battle was fought yesterday, on the 1st heath near Hounslow, between a pugilist, . . . 'Black Jemmy', and a horse-dealer from Shropshire, . . . Gurling." *Morning Chronicle*

Prize fights in the open are illegal, but this adds to the thrill. Last night the secret of the time and place was whispered round the City taverns. A great crowd has been gathering since early morning: sporting gentry (the "Fancy") from town; labourers and farmers from the surrounding country; the rich in carriages and others on foot, are packed round the grass ring.

A roar of excitement goes up as the two men appear, throw off their coats and strip to the waist. Black Jemmy, "who was then teaching the pugilistic art in a neighbouring village", looks faster, but Gurling, the challenger, is thick-set and all muscle. The wager is for 10 guineas but private betting is far higher.

Their seconds lead them to the "scratch"; they shake hands, and begin. The old Broughton rules are simple: bare fists; each round lasts till one or both drop; a minute between rounds; and a fight to the finish.

Some years later Hazlitt saw just such a fight at Hungerford. His essay, "The Fight", says: "There was little cautious sparring—no half-hits—no tapping and trifling— . . . they were almost all knock-down blows: . . . to see two men smashed to the ground, smeared with gore, stunned, senseless, the breath beaten out of their bodies; and then . . . to see them rise up with new strength and courage . . . this is the most astonishing thing of all." Hazlitt describes one blow in the face: "I never saw anything more terrific than his aspect just before he fell. All traces of life, of natural expression, were gone from him. His face was like a human skull, a death's head, spouting blood. The eyes were filled with blood, the nose streamed with blood, the mouth gaped blood."

Today, after fighting one hour, "Gurling was nearly blind, and threw most of his blows away." He fights for 20 more minutes, then falls senseless at Jemmy's feet.

4 MILES WEST OF ANDOVER, ENGLAND

Weyhill Fair is in full swing. Horse-dealers, farmers, wives, quack doctors with pills, servants for hiring, young men with their girls, pickpockets, some soldiers.

"Horses of any figure or bone brought good prices, particularly cart horses." *Brighton Weekly Advertiser.* Cheeses, Farnham hops for beer, raw hides are all for sale. Annual fairs are still the chief means of trade in the country.

ACKWORTH, ENGLAND

William Howitt and two other boys have been caught trespassing. They have been locked up for the night by the keeper, and now they are led in to the squire, who is a Justice. Howitt says:

"'Ay,' said he to a little fat man, his clerk, . . . 'what is the penalty for their offences?'

'The penalty, sir,' replied the clerk, looking at us through his great staring spectacles, 'is the payment of five pounds each, and expenses of warrant, for the poaching . . . in failure of either of these . . . commitment to the house of correction for three months . . .'

"At . . . this sentence . . . we cried, implored, and even danced on the floor for utter agony. . . . But . . . the magistrate, with a . . . loud harsh voice, bade us be silent—and we were silent; all except poor Webb, who, kneeling at the awful man's feet, wrung his hands, and . . . cried, 'Oh, sir! dear sir! do, do forgive us this once; it is my birthday on Sunday, and if you will but forgive us I will send you some of my plum-pudding.'

". . . The worthy man . . . stared at the lad in blank astonishment, and then . . . burst forth into a . . . fit of laughter.

'Your birthday, my boy?—and pray, who are you?'

'O! I am Harry Webb! Harry Webb! sir!'

'Webb? Webb?' said the magistrate; 'what! surely you are not the son of Mr. Webb of Haysford?'

'Oh! I am! I am, sir! . . .'

'. . . Who is this other boy?'

'O, sir! it is Ned Tunstal!'

'Ned Tunstal!' cried the magistrate; '. . . O! now I see it all. Tunstal, I have heard of your doings. I have heard of a certain grey terrier that you keep to disturb all the game in the parish. . . . So you keep a ferret and a net too, to catch rabbits; . . . I'll tell you, Master Tunstal, you will get hanged one of these days.'"

And the boys are set free.

THE GUILDFORD ROAD, ENGLAND

Shouts, cries, and a girl's screams float across the empty fields. "A beautiful young lady eloped . . . with the son of a tradesman near Watling Street. Her father, who is a rich merchant residing near the Kent road, pursued and overtook the fond lovers on their way to Guildford. The young man, after receiving a severe cudgelling from the enraged merchant," said the *Kentish Gazette*, got his way in the end. The fat merchant can't keep up the exertion of a beating, anyway.

KELSO, SCOTLAND

Over the 4 mile Caverton Edge Course, in the first day of the Kelso and Caledonian Hunt Races, Sir H. Williamson's five-year-old, "Honest Starling", has walked away with the 20 guineas sweepstake.

1.30 p.m.

AT SEA, OFF CAPE TRAFALGAR

A wall of smoke; gun flashes; the deafening roar of battle. Lt. Rotely, of the *Victory*'s marines, says: "There was the fire from above, the fire from below, besides the fire from the deck I was upon, the guns recoiling with violence, reports louder than thunder, the decks heaving and the sides straining. I fancied myself in the infernal regions. . . . Lips might move, but orders and hearing were out of the question; everything was done by signs."

The crew of the *Redoutable* are in the rigging ready to board. Captain Lucas writes: "More than two hundred grenades were flung on board her, . . . her decks were strewn with dead and wounded." But his men cannot reach the *Victory*'s higher deck. "I gave the order to cut the supports of the main yard so that it might serve as a bridge." Again the French try to board. Through the smoke the British *Téméraire*, mizen and main topmasts gone, looms up. A "murderous broadside" sweeps the *Redoutable*. "More than 200 of our brave men were killed or wounded by it," says Lucas.

1.40 p.m.

A rending crash as the *Redoubtable* and *Victory*, still hooked, drift into the *Téméraire*. Broadsides are almost muzzle to muzzle. British fire with reduced powder, guns depressed, to avoid shot passing through the *Redoutable* to the other side. Smoke rolls back inboard; gunners work by ear and touch in choking darkness.

The *Redoutable* is a shell. Lucas says: "In the midst of this . . . devastation my splendid fellows who had not been killed, and even the wounded . . . kept cheering 'Vive l'Empereur!'" Then fire breaks out. 12 British row across, climb in the *Redoutable*'s stern ports, and help to fight the flames.

2 p.m.

The French *Fougueux* is also drifting, dismasted. Wreckage litters her side. Her fallen sail is a fire danger, and Pierre Servaux, Master-at-Arms, is ordered overboard to look. He said: "As I clambered from the gangway into the chains one of the enemy fired her whole starboard broadside. The din and concussion were fearful; so tremendous that I almost fell headlong into the sea. Blood gushed from my nose and ears . . ."

The *Victory*, *Redoubtable* and *Téméraire* are driven by the current on to the *Fougueux*. "From the *Téméraire*," says Servaux, "a broadside . . . fired right down into us. It swept our decks clear. Even then our men rallied. With cries of 'à l'arbordage!' repeated all over the ship, some 60 to 80 of them swarmed up on deck, armed with sabres and axes." Again a British three-decker ship is too high to reach from a two-decker, and the French are overwhelmed.

Villeneuve has signalled for his van ships to wear and come to his aid, but too late. His flagship, smashed by continuous broadsides, is helpless. Half his crew is dead or wounded. The ship's barge and boats are crushed under fallen spars: he cannot even leave to hoist his flag on another vessel. "I had to yield to my destiny," he said.

The *Conqueror*'s Log: "At 2.5 the *Bucentaure* struck—sent a boat on board of her to take possession."

Villeneuve surrenders to Marine Captain James Atcherley, who describes the horror between decks: "The dead, thrown back as they fell, lay along the middle of the decks in heaps, and the shot, passing through these, had frightfully mangled the bodies. . . . More than 400 had been killed and wounded, of whom an extraordinary proportion had lost their heads."

2.15 p.m.

Using booms, men on the *Victory* manage at last to push the ship clear of the ruined *Redoutable*. A minute later the *Redoutable*'s mainmast crashes down across the *Téméraire*. Then, says Lucas, "the 2 topmasts of the *Téméraire* came falling on board of us. Our whole poop was stove in, helm, rudder, and stern post all shattered to splinters, all the stern frame, and the decks shot through. All our own guns were either smashed or dismounted by the broadsides of the *Victory* and *Téméraire*. An 18-pounder gun on the lower deck, and a 32-pounder carronade on the forecastle had burst, killing and wounding a great many men. The hull itself was riddled, shot through from side to side; deck beams were shattered; port-lids torn away or knocked to pieces. . . . Everywhere the decks were strewn with dead. . . . Out of a crew of 634 men . . . 300 were killed and 222 wounded."

2.30 p.m.

Certain his wrecked ship will sink anyway, Lucas surrenders.

2.30 p.m.

MAAS SLUYS, ON THE RIVER MEUSE, HOLLAND

Wild fowl scream, and a loose sail flaps like thunder in a freshening wind. By this outpost village, 10 miles down-stream from Rotterdam, a packet for England prepares to put to sea.

One of the passengers is Benjamin Silliman. Since last April, when he sailed from New York, he has been travelling as an agent for Yale College, to buy rare books in Europe for their library. His daily diary will be published in Connecticut in 1820, called "A Journal of Travels".

After a summer of hectic sightseeing in England (it is Silliman who chanced to see Nelson embark at Portsmouth on his last voyage), he came to Holland by this same route in September. Two days ago, in Rotterdam, he ran to earth a fine collection of old books at Lovy and Van Spaan's, of the Wyn Haven. He has bought many, arranging for them to be sent to America after him. He has said "Goodbye" to Mrs. Crabb, an Englishwoman who put him up in Rotterdam (Silliman is not adventurous with food). "She was so obliging as to prepare for us . . . an ample store of provisions for our passage; for we had fared so miserably in coming from England, that we were resolved, not to trust again to the generosity of a Captain."

Holland is officially neutral in the war, though under French control and occupation. The French forbid open travel to England, but "arrangements" can be made.

"The traffic is carried on in this way," explains Silliman. "Dutch boats, commanded, manned, and owned by Dutchmen, clear out of Holland as Prussian, and sail under Prussian colours; they state their destination as being for Embden, a neutral town North of Holland; their papers state that the ship is bound for Embden . . . and the Captain kisses the bible and swears that this is his destination. . . . This thing is so well understood at Rotterdam, that they say, in irony, there are 3 Embdens; great Embden, which is London; little Embden, which is Rotterdam; and the real Embden."

They embarked yesterday at Rotterdam. At Vlaardingen they saw a Dutch fishing-fleet from

Iceland just landed and the quay thronged with women and baskets.

At Maas Sluys the ship (an English cutter captured by the Dutch in the last war) is cleared by customs officers. Silliman's Embden passport is approved, his English letters ignored, by the courteous Dutch official. A German, trying to escape to England without papers (Germany is also under French control), is sent back, weeping, to a French prison. Silliman says: "At ten in the morning we hoisted anchor, and began to float down the river; but . . . a soldier appeared on the wharf, and presenting his musket, threatened to fire into us if we did not instantly drop anchor; after a violent Dutch scolding between him and the captain, which . . . was occasioned by the commandant's having forgotten to give . . . orders to allow us to sail, the thing was satisfactorily explained. . .

"We had a Dutch soldier on board, marching the deck, with gun and bayonet, all the time we were at MAAS SLUYS. A few soldiers are retained in Holland to aid the police, but, almost all the troops . . . are gone to aid the Emperor in this new war.

"When the Dutch sailors sat down to dinner today, they all put their faces to their hats and each one in whispers asked a blessing for himself. I have never before observed the least appearance of religion on board of a ship.—The people of this packet did not swear. A bible lay upon the captain's table . . .

"Between 3 and 4 o'clock we put to sea. . . . The wind was steady, strong, and fair, and the descending shadows of the night, with the rough intervening waves, soon veiled the low-lying fields of Batavia from our view. Sleep made me forget the distressing sickness . . . and when we went on deck in the morning, we were in plain sight of the high chalky cliffs of Old England, which reflected upon us the rays of a bright rising sun."

Silliman sailed just in time. He heard later that his ship was the last to get away to England for many months. A stricter watch stopped the traffic.

2.30 p.m.

Nelson, struck down by a musket-ball, has been carried, in agony, down narrow rope-ways, through gun-decks to the orlop deck below. He has a handkerchief over his face to hide his identity from the crew.

Some wounded men recognize him. They call out: "Mr. Beatty, Lord Nelson is here! Mr. Beatty, the Admiral is wounded." Dr. Beatty, the surgeon, wrote later: "The Surgeon, on looking round, saw the handkerchief fall from his Lordship's face; when the stars on his coat, which had also been covered by it, appeared. Mr. Burke the Purser, and the Surgeon, ran immediately . . . and took him from the arms of the Seamen who had carried him below. . . . They stumbled, but recovered themselves without falling.

"His Lordship was laid upon a bed, stripped of his clothes, and covered with a sheet. While this was effecting, he said to Doctor Scott, 'Doctor, I told you so. Doctor, I am gone.'

"The Surgeon then examined the wound; . . . The ball . . . had penetrated deep into the chest, and had probably lodged in the spine."

Beatty asks Nelson to tell him, if he can, what he feels.

"He replied, that 'he felt a gush of blood every minute within his breast: that he had no feeling in the lower part of his body: and that his breathing was difficult, . . . with very severe pain about . . . the spine where . . . the ball had struck; for,' said he, 'I felt it break my back.'"

Both Beatty and Nelson himself know that nothing can save him, although Beatty tries to keep the other wounded from knowing that their admiral is dying. In the heat and dim light the surgeon's assistants do what they can for the injured. Men cry in pain each time gunfire shakes the deck. Many are out of their misery before the surgeons can reach their turn, bleeding to death on their beds of sail-cloth.

Nelson "now felt an ardent thirst; and frequently called for drink, and to be fanned with paper." Lemonade and wine and water are put to his lips. He

thinks of Hardy and his safety in the battle still raging overhead. "Will no one bring Hardy to me?" he murmurs. "He must be killed: he is surely destroyed."

Hardy has now to act as Commander-in-Chief as his ship still flies the Admiral's flag. He cannot leave the deck before another hour and ten minutes. At last he comes to Nelson, taking his hand. Hardy bends close to hear his words. "How goes the battle? How goes the day with us?" Hardy tells him that they have captured 12 or 14 enemy ships and that no British ship has struck her colours.

Nelson speaks again: "I am a dead man, Hardy. I am going fast: it will be all over with me soon. Come nearer to me. Pray let my dear Lady Hamilton have my hair, and all other things belonging to me."

Hardy tries to comfort his friend, but soon after has to return to the deck.

Nelson tells Beatty he had better leave him and attend the other wounded. "You can do nothing for me," he insists. He tells Beatty that he can no longer move or feel anything below his chest. Beatty examines him again, but the dying man knows it is useless. "Ah, Beatty! I am too certain of it: Scott and Burke have tried it already. You know I am gone." Beatty says: "'My Lord, unhappily for our Country, nothing can be done for you;' and . . . he turned round and withdrew a few steps to conceal his emotions. His Lordship said: 'I know it. I feel something rising in my breast,' putting his hand on his left side, 'which tells me I am gone.'

"Upon the Surgeon's inquiring whether his pain was still very great, he declared, 'it continued so very severe, that he wished he was dead. Yet,' said he in a lower voice, 'one would like to live a little longer, too.'"

Nelson lies silent for a while. For him the cockpit has vanished: his dying brain sees only pictures and perhaps memories of his life. He thinks of his daughter, of the house at Merton, and mostly of Emma. He murmurs: "What will become of her?"

3 p.m.

POLAND STREET, LONDON

"Coming! sir, coming! I've only one pair of hands!" The waiter at the noisy, smoke-filled pub is sweating, rushed off his feet. At 3 chop-houses are still crowded; only working people ate at 12.

One diner plying knife and fork is an art student, Benjamin Robert Haydon. "We used to dine at an ordinary in Poland Street," he wrote, "in a house on the right. You . . . came to the dining-room with a skylight in it. Many French came there, and . . . that old fellow . . . reading the paper with his glasses on."

Nothing too fancy in these places: a cut off the joint or a chop, potatoes and greens, perhaps a fruit-pie. Price about 1/-. In London, one can eat as one likes. "A man," says Silliman, "may dine at the London Coffee House for 1 guinea, or he may descend into a cellar . . . for 3d."

Haydon met Nelson once. "I remember that, after the Battle of the Nile, when quite a child, I was walking with a schoolfellow, near Stonehouse, when a little diminutive man, with a green shade over his eye, a shabby well-worn cocked hat, and buttoned-up undress coat, approached us. . . . My companion said: 'There's Nelson!' 'Let us take off our hats,' said I. We did so, and held them so far out that he could not avoid seeing us, and as he passed he touched his own hat, and smiled."

LONDON BRIDGE

The tide on the turn. Constricted between 19 narrow stone arches, the river roars down a 5 ft. drop to its down-stream level. George Borrow, some years later, tells how a boat "shoots the rapids". His book "Lavengro" says: "Truly tremendous was the roar of the descending waters. . . . As I stood upon the bridge . . . a small boat suddenly

shot through the arch beneath my feet . . . down through that awful water-way, with more than the swiftness of an arrow, shot the boat, or skiff, right into the jaws of the pool. A monstrous breaker curls over the prow—there is no hope; . . . No! the boat, which appeared to have the buoyancy of a feather, skipped over the threatening horror, the boatman . . . elevating one of his skulls in triumph, the man hallooing, and the woman . . . waving her shawl."

ETON COLLEGE, WINDSOR

The Remove has just begun afternoon lessons. A boy of 13 is translating Homer. Lessons are mainly Greek and Latin; no mathematics, science, or modern languages.

"Thus by the beaked ships the Achaeans drew up for battle . . ."

Percy Bysshe Shelley, poet to be, reads on.

54

A FOREST

Throughout England's "green and pleasant land" the Autumn brings country tasks. The woodcutter's axe and saw are already at work in forest clearings. Howitt remembers:

"To see them hewing, stroke after stroke, till down comes the tall tree with a crash and thunder, and the smash of lashing and crushing boughs that resound through the wood. It is curious too, to see in what a little time they will bring down a tree of eighty feet high, and half a yard in diameter . . .

"I have often seen four men at work—three pulling the saw and one pulling it back again—cut down fir-trees of this size in five minutes each. . . . To see them load the heavy trees on their drays, with ropes, and pullies, and levers, and lead them away; or to see them . . . dig their saw-pit in the woods, raise a shelter from the wind over it, . . . and then, with their fire burning cheerfully in cold weather, set to work and saw up the trees into boards and other pieces of timber . . ."

Country boys are gathering acorns. Again Howitt is writing:

"But the grandest sport of all was going of acorn-gathering out in the oak-woods when . . . the great winds come sweeping around, and the dark-brown glossy acorns came rattling down, and lay thickly on the leaf-strewn earth. . . . Everything was wild and excitingly gloomy. The squirrels might be seen springing from bough to bough; the rooks and jackdaws come in crowds to claim their share; and all the old sows in the neighbourhood, at the very first sound of the autumnal blast, had rushed away instinctively to the oak wood. The roaring of the wind was to them as the sound of a trumpet, telling them that acorns were falling in thousands; and if confined in their styes they would scream with rage . . ."

CHELSEA VILLAGE, NEAR LONDON

One of Hannah Smith's stages sets off from the White Horse Inn, Lawrence Street, to the Hercules, Leadenhall Street. They leave daily at 9, 10, 1, 3, 5 and 7. In 40 minutes the country fields are left behind at Westminster, and town begins. Another hour and 20 minutes, and the business man is in the bustle of the City.

3 p.m.

NEAR CORDOBA, SPAIN

A dusty carriage stands outside an inn on the road to Cadiz. Two French soldiers with muskets keep guard, half asleep in the sun. It is hot, though the furnace of summer has died down, even in southern Spain.

In the cool depths of the inn Vice-Admiral Rosily finishes a poor meal with some fruit. His uniform is crumpled, and he eats quickly, as if anxious to be away. His face looks tense and tired; for a month now he has been travelling continuously, at top speed, from Paris. At Madrid he was held up for 3 days by a broken spring, and since leaving there 6 days ago his carriage has lurched and swayed southwards. The road is primitive and he has been warned of bandits.

He carries secret orders from Napoleon to relieve Villeneuve of his command and take over in his place. But he will arrive at Cadiz too late, just 4 days after the allied fleets have fought the battle of Trafalgar.

CADIZ, SPAIN

From city ramparts and house roofs, crowds of Spanish townspeople keep an anxious watch. All afternoon the faint booming of gun-fire has blown in on the sea wind; and out on the horizon, to the south-west, a distinct smoke cloud spreads steady and ominous. People think of friends, sons, husbands who are in the battle, and wonder if they will return.

The echo of gun-fire can occasionally be heard far inland, beyond Medina Sidonia, across half Andalusia, as far as the caves at Ronda. Gibraltar hears nothing, but outside Tangier some shepherd boys sit on a hillside listening to the strange sound of thunder that seems to be coming in from the sea.

AT SEA, OFF CAPE TRAFALGAR

In the doomed allied fleet, everywhere acts of obstinate, gallant, daring courage. Churruca lies on the deck of the *San Juan*, dead; his ship surrendered, half his crew out of action.

The French *Aigle* has been terribly battered. Running into the *Bellerophon*, her crew tried repeatedly to board until the British ship shot herself free with successive broadsides. Then the *Revenge* ran into the *Aigle* and again with 2 broadsides shook herself clear. Crippled now, the French ship drifts towards the *Defiance*.

Log of *Defiance*: "At 3.10 run alongside of her . . . —took possession of her quarter-deck and poop— struck the French colours and hoisted English—her people still firing from her tops, forecastle, and lower-deck." Intense musket and pistol-fire drives the British off. "3.35 the boarders were ordered from the *Aigle*, cast off the lashing, and hauled off about pistol-shot distance, and engaged her again. About 4 they called for quarter .-. .''

3.30 p.m.

ON BOARD THE *Victory*

The echoes of firing, and sometimes of cheers as an enemy ship surrenders, filter down to the dim stuffiness of the cockpit. Surgeons and assistants are at their gruesome work: pressing leather gags in mens' mouths, sawing through shattered limbs, pouring wine down throats to revive men who have fainted. Midshipman Westphal is lying with a head wound, with Nelson's coat rolled up as a pillow. Later, he will write: "Several of the bullions of the epaulet were found to be so firmly glued into my hair" by the dried blood that they have to be cut off and left in his hair.

By Westphal's side lies Nelson himself, dying fast from internal bleeding.

Hardy comes a second time. Nelson, although much weaker now, manages to think of the dangerous shoals lying near. He speaks with sudden energy: " '*Anchor*, Hardy, *anchor!*' To this the Captain replied: 'I suppose, my Lord, Admiral Collingwood will now take upon himself the direction of affairs.' 'Not while I live, I hope, Hardy!' cried the dying Chief; and at that moment endeavoured . . . to raise himself from the bed. 'No, . . . do *you* anchor, Hardy.' Captain Hardy then said: 'Shall *we* make the signal, Sir?' 'Yes,' answered His Lordship; 'for if I live, I'll anchor.' "

Dr. Beatty continues the story:

"He then told Captain Hardy, 'he felt that in a few minutes he should be no more;' adding in a low tone, 'Don't throw me overboard, . . . Kiss me, Hardy.' The Captain . . . kissed his cheek; when His Lordship said, 'Now I am satisfied.' . . . Hardy stood for a minute or two, . . . then knelt down again, and kissed His Lordship's forehead. His Lordship said: 'Who is that?' The Captain answered: 'It is Hardy;' to which His Lordship replied, 'God bless you, Hardy!' After this . . . Captain Hardy . . . returned to the quarter-deck, having spent about eight minutes in this his last interview with his dying friend."

3 p.m.

SANSANDING, WEST AFRICA

A blinding tropic sun makes the air tremble above the River Niger. On the caked mud on the bank a great canoe is building. Some English and Scotsmen, half in rags, beat off the flies as they slowly haul new timbers into position. The heat is like an oven; touching stone or iron will blister one's hands, and even wood is painful to hold. Several men are weak with fever: only their leader, a 6-ft. Scot, seems to give them strength to carry on.

He is Mungo Park, 34 years old, scientist, botanist, doctor. Sir Joseph Banks, thousands of miles away, in London, has sent him a second time to try to trace the route of the Niger.

Britain, the "Nation of Shopkeepers", is also a nation of explorers, intent on finding new markets and routes for trade. Gold is known to come from somewhere near the fabulous city of Timbuktu; there is evidence of civilization in the unknown interior; and there is the unsolved puzzle of the Niger, the great river flowing north-east, *away* from the sea.

Some think it may connect with the Congo, or perhaps lead to some huge inland lake, or even cross the breadth of Africa to join the waters of the Nile. No one suspects that it turns and finally runs southwards into the Gulf of Benin.

For nearly a year Park's expedition has fought its way steadily inland. From early June, monsoon rains have delayed the overland trek to Marraboo where, in August, the party set out in canoes on the Niger.

For the last 3 weeks, the survivors have been at Sansanding. On 2 October Park wrote in his diary that two more soldiers died from fever and dysentery. "During the night the wolves carried away Garland, the door of the hut where he died being left open."

This is the kingdom of Bambarra, ruled by Mansong from his capital at Sego. The rulers are Arabs, the people mixed Arabs and Africans. Sansanding is a busy town of 11,000 people. All the houses, even the Moorish mosques, are built of mud. Park writes that, despite the heat, "the market is crowded from morning to night." In the dense shadow of thick grass mats, scores of stalls show the brilliant colours of their merchandise. They sell beads, indigo, wood ashes, cloth, tobacco, sulphur, lead, copper, silver rings, Moroccan silk, salt. "A large butcher's stall . . . is in the centre . . . and as good and fat meat sold every day as any in England."

Cowrie shells are used for money. 5,000 shells equal £1; a slave costs 40,000 shells, a fat cow 15,000.

Park's greatest need is a new boat. Mansong has cheated by selling a canoe half-rotten. Park sends again to the king. Park's diary says: "I sent 2 blunderbusses, 2 fowling pieces, 2 pair of pistols, and 5 unservicable muskets; requesting in return that Mansong would either send a proper canoe, or permit me to purchase one." Yesterday it arrived, but still "half of it was very much decayed and patched." The only answer is to join together the separate halves which are sound. After 18 more days of hard work the new ship will be christened H.M. Schooner *Joliba*. On 16 November they will sail into the Kingdom of Haoussa.

The Chief of Yaour will keep the presents Park sends for the King, and this will cost Park his life. His Arab slave, Amadi Fatouma, will live to tell the story:

"The next morning early the King sent an army to a village called Boussa. . . . There is before this village a rock across the whole breadth of the river . . . there is a large opening . . . in the form of a door, which is the only passage for the water to pass through. . . . This army went and took possession of the top of this opening. Mr. Park . . . attempted to pass. The people began to attack him, throwing lances, pikes, arrows and stones. . . . Two of his slaves at the stern of the canoe were killed . . . being overpowered by numbers . . . and unable to keep up the canoe against the current . . . Mr. Park took hold of one of the white men, and jumped into the water . . . and they were drowned."

3.15 p.m.

13 MILES EAST OF ULM, GERMANY

In pale sunshine, Napoleon's coach is entering the desolate town of Leipheim, 9 miles out of Elchingen on the Augsburg road. A cavalry-troop commander rides by the door; mounted guards in front and behind. Behind them march regiments of foot Guards.

In the coach itself sits a huddled figure, well muffled in a plain grey coat. Napoleon has no eyes for the Danube just 300 yards to his left. He is wrapped in his own thoughts, his expression sombre. His face is strained with fatigue. Never a big eater, he has snatched only the briefest snack before leaving Elchingen. His mind is probably running on figures. Every morning he demands full accounts of men and casualties. He "always had a strange pleasure in receiving these reports. He used to read them through with delight . . . his marvellous memory grasped all their details," wrote Baron de Méneval. He loves dictating bulletins. One proclamation, made this morning, runs:

Soldiers of the Grand Army

In 15 days we have made a campaign. . . . We have chased the troops of the House of Austria from Bavaria. . . . Of 100,000 men . . . 60,000 are prisoners . . . So great a result has not weakened us above 1500 *hors de combat*. But we shall not stop here. . . . We shall make that Russian army . . . undergo the same fate. . . . My soldiers are my children.

In fact, Napoleon thinks of his soldiers only as units or machines. Two years from now, on the field of Eylau, he will be seen turning over a French corpse with his foot, and be heard to say, "Small change!" He has said, "Friendship is only a word. I care for nobody."

He was in love once, but certainly not with his wife Josephine. He confided to General Bertrand: "Actually, I married Josephine only because I thought she had a large fortune. . . . In short, it was a good stroke of business for me."

But his personal magnetism, his victories, the legend of his name, inspire his troops with a fierce loyalty. The men of the Guard are proud to be his escort.

The confusion is appalling. On either side of the road, struggling in mud, the rearmost columns of Marshal Oudinot's grenadiers are being overtaken. Wagons, cannon, limbers, spare horses spread to each side to let the Guard through. Oudinot's columns, 6 miles long, are making south-east in pursuit of Archduke Ferdinand's main Austrian army in the Tyrol.

Coming back down the road in the opposite direction are unending, scattered groups of Austrian prisoners. Tens of thousands, taken from a huge circle of French victories around Ulm: Nördlingen, Neresheim, Langenau, to the north; Donauwörth, Augsburg, Günzburg, Haslach, to the east: they are straggling westwards towards France. French soldiers watch and march with them. Everyone is half-starved. The Foot Guard themselves are exhausted. Uniforms are soaked, muddy to the thighs. For eight weeks the men have been on the move. They have hardly stopped since leaving Boulogne, 440 miles away. Once they covered 130 miles in four days and nights to catch up

with Napoleon's coach at Nördlingen. They linked arms to stop falling. Some fell asleep while marching. Grenadiers have tents; the rest sleep in the open—for the past week in cold rain and gales. At Elchingen they supported the attack on the bridge by General Murat's 6th corps. From the 15th, when Napoleon made his headquarters in the Abbey, they bivouacked in the ruined villages of Haslach and Thalfingen.

Each guardsman is laden like a mule. Spare clothes, shoes, sleeping-bag and biscuit rations go in his heavy, fur-covered pack. Around it hang great-coat, bearskin bonnet, mess tins, hat. Belts and straps hold cartridge pouches, bayonet, 32-inch sabre and 50-inch musket.

Napoleon's route lies east. Augsburg tomorrow, Vienna on 15 November, a crushing victory over the Russians at Austerlitz on 2 December. And always the Guard will follow, even to the end at Waterloo. . . .

3.20 p.m.

VIENNA, AUSTRIA

Just 300 miles east of Napoleon.

At the Theater an der Wien, a short, thick-set figure conducts rehearsal. His gestures are violent and he has a cruel tongue for any mistakes. The opera "Fidelio" is within one month of its opening. The conductor—and composer—is Ludwig van Beethoven, now at the height of his success. He worked on the score during the summer in the country, but he is now installed again at Vienna. As well as his own rooms at Mölkerbastei on the old ramparts of the town, he has a year's free lodging at the theatre included in his fee.

Beethoven, like many artists, saw Napoleon in the beginning as a star of light in a dark, oppressed world. Last year he inscribed his great Third Symphony to Napoleon Bonaparte. Then he heard that Napoleon was crowned Emperor. It was Beethoven's pupil, Ries, who brought the news. He said: "Beethoven . . . flew into a rage and cried out '. . . Now he, too, will trample on all the rights of man, and . . . become a tyrant!' . . . He took hold of the title-page by the top, tore it in two, and threw it on the floor." He renamed it "Sinfonia Eroica".

"Fidelio", the opera glorifying man's freedom, will open in 30 days' time in a Vienna full of French troops, and to an audience of French officers. The French will be amused by the flying hair and the barbaric look of the famous Beethoven, but in a city disrupted by war the opera will flop.

At the Café Hügelmann they are playing billiards. The game is all the rage in Vienna. There are tournaments, champions, even a "University" of billiards. Despite an autumn chill in the air, the tables in the large garden outside are crowded. When the weather is fine, Monday, or "Blue Monday" as it is called, is more or less a holiday.

Vienna is a mixture of East and West and its streets are full of all kinds of people. Certainly, one can hear most tongues of Europe at Hügelmann's, if one waits. From its riverside garden one can see the boats on the Danube, colourful against the brown water, as they pass under the Ferdinandsbrücke, which joins the city to the suburb of Leopoldstadt.

People drink their coffee, admire the Greek or Turkish dress of the sailors, gossip, and try to forget the distant war.

PARIS, FRANCE

Under Napoleon, France is ruled as a family affair. His elder brother Prince Joseph is head of state while Napoleon is abroad at war. Joseph has just presided over today's meeting of the Senate. A routine meeting, mainly paying tribute to François Cacault, Senator, who died on Friday last.

Boulevards are thronged, cafés full. At the Pavillon de Hanovre, by the corner of the Boulevard des Italiens and the Rue Louis-le-Grand, women of leisure show off their latest dresses—high waisted and flowing in the classic style—while many young men are in officer's uniform. They drink coffee, talk scandal, and find Veloni's ice-cream as delicious as ever.

By the corner of the Boulevard and Rue de Richelieu the roulette room at the Café Frascati already boasts a sprinkling of die-hard gamblers. The galleries of the Palais Royal are full of strollers: Grenadier reservists, officers, fashionable young women. At the end is the Café Borel, where they treated Sergeant Jean Coignet—now with Napoleon's Guard, on the road to Augsburg—to free punch, when he walked in with a brand-new cross of the Legion of Honour on his tunic.

BRIGHTON, ENGLAND

"The Prince continues to enliven Brighton with his presence, and the town may truly be said to be still very gay." *Brighton Weekly Advertiser*

A low sun reflects from the Channel in pinpoints of silver. Out to sea, scattered sails; and hull down on the horizon, a British man-o'-war.

The Steyne promenade is crowded. "The Prince of Wales, Counts Starhemberg, Barons Linsengen and Ebben, Count Beaujolais, Lord and Lady Melbourne, Lord and Lady Leslie, Earl and Countess of Clarent, were all on the Steyne." *Daily Advertiser*

Baron Ebben has had a busy morning. As the Prince's adjutant, and because he can't swim, he has tested a new life-saving machine. He was afloat for ½ hour at the 11.30 high tide. Bystanders, including the Prince, were gratified to see the test successful.

Brighton is still small (18 main streets, about 7,000 residents), but becoming more fashionable each year. The Prince has bought a country house which will become the Royal Pavilion, and nearly all the main houses let lodgings. For some years now, in the summer, wooden changing-huts, on wheels, have been seen on the beach. But except for Baron Ebben, few people were swimming today....

3.30 p.m.

Here on the American west coast, the time is 8 hours behind Europe's. It is now 7.30 in the morning.

On either side of the river rise barren cliffs, rocky overhangs, scattered pines. A pale sun shines, but at this height a mountain wind blows chill. The foaming water pours in a series of rapids between huge fallen boulders, roaring and echoing like thunder along the gorge. First one canoe, then a second, plunges headlong into a cloud of spray. It seems they must be smashed to pieces on the rocks and their men drowned. But by some miracle they dart out, unharmed, into the frothing water below.

In one month's time they will reach Fort Clatsop at the mouth of the Columbia—the first Europeans ever to cross the American continent from Louisiana to the Pacific Ocean.

For years traders and fur-trappers have tried to find a route across the Rocky Mountains to the western coast. When Napoleon, in 1803, sold the French colony of Louisiana to the young American Republic, Thomas Jefferson, the President, decided to send his secretary, Captain Meriwether Lewis, to open a westwards route, with Captain William Clark as second-in-command. 29 Americans, 14 French and half-breed interpreters and guides, Clark's Negro slave York, and an Indian woman, Sacajawea, all set off from Camp River Dubois, on the Missouri, on 14 May, 1804.

The trail has been hard and slow, always in Indian territory. Throughout 1804 they journeyed across the great Mid-West plains. The land was rich in game: once they reckoned a herd of buffalo, spreading as far as the eye could reach, to number 300,000. At Christmas they built a wooden fort for shelter among the Mandan Indians of North Dakota. Setting out again in the April of this year, they trekked still westwards.

Only 5 weeks before this, they crossed the highest part of the great divide of the Rockies. Lewis wrote, on 15 September: "... encamped on the top of the mountains near a Bank of old Snow about 3 ft. deep ... we melted the snow to drink, and cooked our horse flesh to eat."

The trail became more arduous, descending "steep hillsides, obstructed with fallen timber." Horses died, and when their flesh was eaten there remained no food at all. The men nearly starved.

A week later they reached the Clearwater River. They built canoes and sailed down this into the Snake River and finally into the Columbia.

The party can only eat what it finds: yesterday they shot 2 speckled gulls and some wild duck.

Captain Clark, 35 years old, a tough Virginian soldier, veteran of many battles, describes today in his diary:

October 21st Monday 1805

"A verry cool morning wind from the S.W. we set out verry early ... passd a Small Island at 5½ miles a large one 8 miles in the middle of the river ... and Eight Lodges of nativs opposit its Lower point ... we came too at those lodges, bought some wood and brackfast, Those people recived us with great kindness ... we got from those people a fiew pounded roos [roots] fish and Acorns of white oake ...

"... at 2 miles lower passed a rapid large rocks stringing into the river of large Size ... here we halted a fiew minits to examine the rapid before we entered it ... put out all who Could not Swim to walk around ...

"... a-little below is a bad rapid which is bad crouded with hugh [huge] rocks scattered in every Direction ... emence piles of rocks appears as if Sliped from the clifts ...

"... & below this ... comences a rapid which is crouded with large rocks in every direction ... we halted at a Lodge to examine those noumerous Islands of rock ... great numbs of Indians came in canoes to View us at this place, after passing this rapid which we accomplished without loss; winding between the hugh rocks for about 2 miles."

They will reach Louisiana again on 23 September, 1806, after crossing the continent both ways, in an expedition of 8,000 miles, lasting 2 years and 4 months.

3.40 p.m.

THE ATLANTIC COAST, U.S.A.

2,800 miles east of Lewis and Clark. The time is 5 hours behind Europe's. Here, it is 10.40 a.m.

News crosses the continent slowly. A letter dated 25 May, from Illinois, has just reached the *Republican Advocate*. It says:

"Six of Captain Lewis and Clark's men have arrived in St. Louis . . . they were just about to . . . pursue their journey to the Pacific Ocean."

LONG ISLAND SOUND, NEW YORK

Rich fishing grounds lie off the Atlantic seaboard. Joshua Perry is hauling nets from his boat. In 2 days' time he will catch "three sharks . . . called shovel-nose . . . the largest . . . eleven feet long. On opening him, many detatched parts of a man were found in his body, which were collected and buried. There was also found a striped cotton shirt, patched in the sides and sleeves, with bright striped pieces." *Vermont Centinel*

PHILADELPHIA, PENNSYLVANIA

Both in this city and in New York, reports the *Philadelphia Daily Advertiser*, ". . . the Malignant Fever, which, during the two months past, was permitted to maintain an uncontrolled empire . . ." is past its peak. Citizens who had fled to the countryside have begun to return home. Tomorrow the Philadelphia Board of Health will announce no further deaths, and only 16 people still fevered in hospital. "The streets are again crowded."

BOSTON, MASSACHUSETTS

A bustling city, and a sea-port for trade from all over the world. In the outer waters of the harbour many ships lie at anchor, silent, separated, with no boats near. They fly a yellow flag at the masthead.

The dreaded yellow fever which has devastated the mainland was probably carried in from Africa or the East, but until the epidemic is really over all ships must anchor for quarantine. 40 days must elapse since each ship last left a foreign port before any of its crew or passengers can come ashore. Their captains curse at the delay, but orders are strict.

At the harbour wharves and docks some ships are just in, their quarantine finished and having been passed as clean by the doctors. Everywhere booms and cranes are unloading rich cargoes. Men shout and sweat to make up for lost time.

The *Independent Chronicle* lists ships in today. The *Glide* from Bordeaux, the *Thomas* from Leghorn, the *Industry* from Puerto Rico, the *Hercules* from Amsterdam, the *Betsy* from Martinique, and others. . . . The *Juno* is about to sail for Calcutta, India. In a few days the *Liberty* is due off for New York.

Quayside warehouses are crammed with goods from abroad. Jamaica rum and spirits, Bordeaux wine, sugars and China tea, molasses, French gloves and shawls, English cottons and wool cloth, candles . . .

At C. Hayward's office the buyers are tasting some new Fayal wine. 6 huge barrels, or "pipes", each of 130 gallons, are to be auctioned at noon. A brand-new schooner, 124 tons, "completely rigged for sea" glistens in its new paint at Hewes Wharf at Fort Hill, where it is up for sale.

At the Boston theatre Mr. Cooper is at rehearsal. Even without his black greasepaint he promises to be a fine Othello tonight for the opening of Shakespeare's tragedy. The audience will get its money's worth: after "Othello" there will follow "an afterpiece, called Who's the Dupe."

SANDY BAY, MASSACHUSETTS

Recent storms have wrecked many ships.

"The wreck of a schooner . . . was fallen in with, 17th inst., about half a league N.E. of Cape Ann Lights . . . her foremast carried away. . . . She is loaded with wood and shingles . . ." *Salem Register*

SALEM, MASSACHUSETTS

A worse danger than storms to American sailors is capture on the high seas, and forced service in a British man-o'-war. Feeling runs high. The *Salem Register* reports that, to escape capture, American seamen must have a birth-certificate as well as a Protection Order signed by the American Customs. But, it argues, "why should our seamen be compelled to furnish themselves with protections at all? . . . It would not surprise us much, if the English wished to establish Customs Houses in the United States, . . . compelling our ships and seamen to make entry and clear out before their own officers . . .

". . . It is full time the English Government should tell us whether sugar and coffee are . . . to be added to the list of contraband articles . . . and whether we are to be permitted to carry on any trade with France and Holland or Spain in future . . . as it is now, we are no more allowed a free trade, than we were previous to the revolution. . . ."

GOSPORT, VIRGINIA

"It is certain that our Government is determined to add six 74's to our infant navy; the building of one of them . . . is immediately to take place at the Navy Yard, Gosport." *Thomas's Massachusetts Spy*. They will soon be fighting British ships. The last war between America and Britain is only 7 years hence.

WORCESTER, MASSACHUSETTS

Inland, New England is a country of farms, woods and orchards. An advertisement, dated today, will appear in the *Massachusetts Spy* on Wednesday.

For Sale, in main street of Worcester, . . . a Mansion house, and good, well furnished Barn, including a convenient place for carriages—a large Woodhouse, and other outhouses—a good Well—an excellent and productive Garden—together with about ¾ of an acre of land. . . . There is an avenue on each side, through which teams, loaded with wood etc., may pass round the House. There is a handsome Front Yard, planted with shade trees, shrubs etc.

WORCESTER, MASSACHUSETTS

In a trading nation money can be powerful, but the democratic spirit of Americans won't tolerate fraud. The *Massachusetts Spy* thinks that Thomas Ward, the new Sheriff, has forged his credentials. "We do not know who furnished . . . documents to prove . . . 24 towns in favour of the nomination, but we are confident that it . . . will prove . . . to be only from 24 of Ward's minions. . . . We are confident that the day is not far

distant . . . when the appointment will be regretted by Thousands."

Ward hits back in a letter reaching the newspaper office today: "Isaiah Thomas Jun., strike my name from the list for the *Spy*, for I do not feal dispos'd to take your PARTIAL, ABUSIVE, RASCAL-LY PAPER any longer,

THOS. W. WARD."

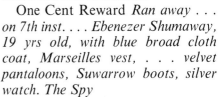

WORCESTER

Some are less fortunate.

One Cent Reward Ran away . . . on 7th inst. . . . Ebenezer Shumaway, 19 yrs old, with blue broad cloth coat, Marseilles vest, . . . velvet pantaloons, Suwarrow boots, silver watch. The Spy

In all countries, apprentices are little more than slaves.

BURLINGTON, VERMONT

Compared with England, America punishes its criminals lightly. Alfa Bucknam is before the Supreme County Court. He admits to "burning the building of Levi Barnard, esq., in Lunenburgh."

"The court sentenced him to stand in the pillory two succeeding days, one hour each day, and to be whipped twenty-five lashes." *Peacham Paper*, reported by the *Vermont Centinel*

The *Centinel* also is advertising for *A postrider wanted. Any person . . . may hear of a good route by applying at this office.* 53 years after Franklin tapped electricity by a kite, letters still go by horseback.

And it will be 8 more weeks before the news of Trafalgar will reach America.

3.45 p.m.

AT SEA, OFF CAPE TRAFALGAR

Nearly all British ships have by now reached the centre of battle. The *Belleisle*, second in line to the *Royal Sovereign*, has been surrounded and fired on from all sides for nearly three hours. Below decks, said an eye-witness afterwards, "the smoke accumulated more and more thickly, stagnating . . . so densely as to . . . blot out the men at the guns. . . . The guns had to be trained . . . by . . . orders passed down from above." Men can hear only "the crash of the shot smashing through the rending timbers, and . . . the hoarse bellowings of the captains of the guns . . . calling out to the survivors, 'Close up there! Close up!'"

Already 33 officers and men lie dead, 93 wounded. All three mainmasts with their rigging and sails, the bowsprit, figure-head, boats, and even the anchors have been shot away. "We lay a mere hulk, covered in wreck and rolling with the swell," said the same eye-witness.

"At this hour a two-decked ship was seen . . . we had scarcely seen British colours since one o'clock . . . and it is impossible to express our emotion as an alteration of the stranger's course displayed the white ensign to our sight."

Another British ship, the *Swiftsure*, passes close by the *Belleisle*'s stern. In answer to the *Swiftsure*'s cheers someone on the *Belleisle* holds up a Union Jack tied to a pike, while a white ensign droops from the stump of the mizen mast.

Log of *Belleisle*: "Ceased firing, and turned the hands up to clear the wreck. Sent a boat and took possession of the Spanish 80-gun Ship, *Argonauta*. . . . At 4.15 the *Naiad* came down and took us in tow . . ."

The *Intrépide* is one of Dumanoir's van squadron. Her Captain, Infernet, is a formidable giant, "as tall as a drum major, and as stout as a Benedictine monk." He is uneducated, an ex-cabin boy from Toulon. Without waiting for signals, he has had his ship hauled round by a boat (since there was not enough wind), and has sailed down into the thick of the battle around the *Bucentaure*.

"He wanted, he said, to rescue Villeneuve and take

him on board, and then to rally the ships that were still in a fit state to fight. . . . He would not have it said that the *Intrépide* had quitted the battle while she could still fight a gun or haul a sail. It was noble madness. . . ."

Infernet's report says: "Half an hour after, I was attacked by 3 [ships] and very near; at 3 o'clock by 4; and 15 minutes later by 5. I was firing both broadsides and even reserve cannon, the fight was the most obstinate. . . . Later, I was surrounded by 7 ships, which all fired down on me."

Nelson still lies, barely living, on the orlop deck of the *Victory*, below the water-line. Dr. Scott, the Chaplain, and Mr. Burke hold raised the end of the sail-cloth mattress, keeping Nelson's shoulders lifted to ease a little his pain. His face is white and sunken.

Dr. Beatty describes the end: "Lord Nelson now desired . . . his Steward to turn him upon his right side; which being effected, his Lordship said: 'I wish I had not left the deck, for I shall soon be gone.'" Nelson "afterwards became very low . . . and his voice faint. He

said to Doctor Scott, 'Doctor, I have *not* been a *great* sinner,' and after a short pause, '*Remember*, that I leave Lady Hamilton and my Daughter Horatia as a legacy to my Country: . . . never forget Horatia.' . . . then, with evident increase of pain, . . . pronounced distinctly these last words: 'Thank God, I have done my duty.' . . .

"His Lordship became speechless in about fifteen minutes after Captain Hardy left him. When he had remained speechless about five minutes, his . . . Steward went to the Surgeon. . . . The Surgeon . . . knelt down by his side, and took up his hand; which was cold, and the pulse gone from the wrist. On . . . feeling his forehead, which was likewise cold, His Lordship opened his eyes, looked up, and shut them again. The Surgeon again left him, and returned to the wounded . . . but was not absent five minutes before the Steward announced to him that 'he believed His Lordship had expired.' The Surgeon returned, and found that . . . His Lordship had breathed his last, at thirty minutes past four o'clock."

5 p.m.

ROEHAMPTON, ENGLAND

"The Earl of Buckingham entertains a large dinner-party this day at his seat in Roehampton." *Morning Chronicle*

Formal afternoon dinners begin late. English gentry eat a bread-and-butter-breakfast, a huge dinner, no afternoon tea, but a late-night supper. Dinner this evening is turtle soup, oysters, salmon and trout, pheasant, roast beef and mutton, fruit-pies, custards and ices. Wines are claret, Madeira, port and finally brandy. Eating goes on until 8.

NEWGATE STREET, LONDON

The heavy prison doors grate open, and Thomas Flood, Robert Hinds, and Edward Williams walk out into the dusk. They have been imprisoned in Newgate for debt; at last friends have found them money and now they are free.

The prison records list 278 debtors for this October. Many, for want of money, will die here. They sleep on wood boards, get 2 lb. of dry bread every 2 days, a very little meat once a week, and that is all. Until they can pay their debts and gaoler's fees they endure their days and years, miserably crowded, in the "Common Side".

Some debtors do have cash. 13/6d entry fee and 2/6d weekly buys a bed in the "Master's Side". For 2 guineas entrance and 10/6d a week one can be sure of distinguished company in the select "State Side". With daily visits and their own food brought in, life is not too bad for people here.

In the dark cells of the "Criminal Side" conditions are worst of all. Burglary, forgery, passing false money, murder: these crimes are punished by death. Today, 24 convicts are under sentence to hang. Three of them, Richard Harding, William Cubitt and Mary Parnell, will be hanged on 13 November. The others will be transported instead, for 14 years or for life, to Australia.

64 others, sentenced to transportation, lie waiting in other cells. They will be sent to ships on 20 and 24 December. Among them are 6 children imprisoned for theft. Mary Berry, aged 16; Rebecca Reason and Catherine Gready, both 15; Mary Marney and John Carter, 14; and tiny Sarah Sullivan, 11; all will be transported. They have spent 6 months lying in Newgate; in just 7 weeks' time they will be sent, in irons, on board the *Alexander* prison ship at Longreach, on the Thames, by the bleak Dartford marshes.

CLAPHAM, NEAR LONDON

At a private house, the port is passing round after dinner. One guest is a clergyman whom Silliman saw:

"His hand, which was at first attended by such a tremulous motion . . . that he could only with difficulty carry the glass to his mouth, became steadier as his nerves began to be stimulated with wine, till . . . he sunk into a slumber. . . . The conversation turned on Bonaparte. . . . At this crisis the Doctor lifted his heavy eye-lids, and with a voice almost as sullen and unexpected as if it had come from a tomb, exclaimed, 'What, Bonaparte come to England—he invade the country—a damned lamp-lighting scoundrel!'"

DERBYSHIRE, ENGLAND

"There are children that are set to pick up a few pence by watching a gate, to open it for travellers," writes William Howitt. "I know a gate on a distant heath where a little girl is commonly to be found. She goes there after breakfast, takes her dinner, and stays till night."

BOW STREET MAGISTRATE'S COURT, LONDON, ENGLAND

"If these charges be proved, the prisoner must hang." Sir Richard Ford, the magistrate, speaks solemnly. The youth in the dock bursts into tears.

The first case in the evening's session is being heard.

"A youth, aged about 18, . . . was brought up for the first time, . . . under numerous charges of forgery. He was in a midshipman's uniform, double-ironed, and belongs to one of H.M. ships of war lately arrived in Yarmouth." *The Times*

The boy had been an apprentice, got into bad ways, and was sent to sea in the hope the Navy would make a man of him. The cure failed. On his first shore-leave he has stolen and forged cheques in his old Master's name.

Sir Richard says that "the prisoner was in the hands of the prosecutor"—the boy's Master. But the boy is young, of a good family, has been in the war at sea, and the magistrate is sympathetic. To avoid the harshness of the law—a convicted forger must hang—he suggests the tradesman makes a lesser charge, which will mean merely exile.

LITTON MILL, NEAR TIDESWELL, ENGLAND

Robert Blincoe lies bleeding on the filthy floor of the cotton mill, behind his stretching-frame. The blow that felled him was only one of many today from his overseer, Robert Woodward, who says he has been working slowly. Woodward is a sadist who delights in torture.

"If he made a kick at Blincoe, so great was his strength, it commonly lifted him off the floor. . . . He and others used to throw rollers, one after another, at the poor boy, aiming at his head . . . and nothing delighted the savages more than to see Blincoe stagger . . . and the blood rushing out in a stream. . . . In consequence of such wounds, his head was over-run with vermin . . ."

Like the other boy and girl apprentices, he is always half-starving. Robert Brown, who met Blincoe in later life, published his "Memoir" in the *Lion Magazine*. "If Blincoe happened to see any fresh cabbage leaves, potato or turnip parings, thrown out upon a dung-hill, he ran down with a can full of sweepings, as an excuse, and as he threw that dirt on the dung-hill, he would eagerly pick the other up, and carry it in his shirt . . . into the mill." He also managed to steal dumplings sometimes from the pigs-swill.

One of Blincoe's tortures is to have his teeth filed to a point. "I do this," said Woodward, "to sharpen thy teeth, that thou mayest eat thy Sunday dinner the better." Many apprentices die from wounds and disease. "So great had

the mortality been, that Mr. Needham (the mill owner) felt it advisable to divide the burials, some in Toddington, some in Tideswell church yards." To replace the deaths yearly drafts of children are sent from parish work-houses. In the mills they will be prisoners, sometimes treated worse than animals, until they are 21 or die before then.

Robert Brown wrote: "No savageness in human nature, that has existed on earth, has been paralleled by . . . the English Cotton-spinning Mills."

YORKSHIRE, ENGLAND

A pedlar stands at a cottage door. In the gathering night it is difficult to see colour; he goes in to the fire-side while the woman chooses a penny ribbon. Outside, his horse, carrying all he possesses in saddle-bags, waits for him.

4.30 p.m.

Strong current towards shore.

Everywhere desolation, ships sinking, fires. Nearly all allied ships surrendered.

Log of *Mars*: "At 4, French Commander-in-Chief came on board with his retinue." Of the other 5 allied Admirals, Dumanoir is cut off, Magon is dead, and Alava, Gravina and Cisneros all wounded. 4 flagships are prizes.

At 4.30 the French *Achille* is on fire in the fore-top. Log of *Prince*: "Gave her 3 broadsides which cut away her masts and set her on fire." The flaming fore-top falls inboard, fire catches hold in the waist, soon the ship is in flames. Men jump from her ports into the sea. The British cease firing. "Out boats to save the crew." Naked men begin to be pulled into the British boats. The fire sets off some of *Achille*'s guns, left loaded.

A woman is trapped in the ship's lower deck. She came from Flanders and refused to leave her husband. At Cadiz, she disguised as a seaman, and is serving in the fore-magazine passage. Ladders to the main deck are shot away; the fire burns down towards her. Her name is Jeanette. A Lieutenant on the *Revenge* tells her story:

"She remained wandering to and fro upon the lower deck, among the . . . dying and the slain, until the guns from the main deck actually fell through the burnt planks. Her only refuge, then, was the sea, and the poor creature scrambled out of the gun-room port, and, by the help of the rudder chains, reached the back of the rudder. . . . At length the lead which lined the rudder-trunk began to melt, and to fall upon her, and her only means of avoiding this was to leap overboard."

She is picked up, naked, by a boat's crew from the *Belleisle*. "One supplied her with trowsers, another stripped off his jacket, and threw it over her. . . . She was much burned about the neck, shoulders, and legs, by the molten lead, and when she reached the *Pickle* was more dead than alive."

Tomorrow, on the *Revenge*, she will be treated as a guest. "The poor creature was almost famished with hunger. One of the Lieutenants gave her a piece of sprigged blue muslin, which he had obtained from a Spanish prize, and two new checked shirts were supplied by the purser. . . . Being a dressmaker, she made herself a sort of jacket . . . and the purser's shirts . . . into an outer petticoat . . . white stockings and a pair of the chaplain's shoes were on her feet." 4 days later she will joyfully find her husband, alive, among the prisoners.

4. 45 p.m.

Gravina's flagship, *Principe de Asturias*, gets the French frigate *Thémis* to take her in tow. She signals 11 uncaptured ships to follow her to Cadiz.

5.8 p.m.

Infernet is held down, while his surviving officers surrender to overwhelming odds. His ship, the *Intrépide*, is the last French ship to surrender. He is taken, with his 10-year-old son, a midshipman, on board the *Orion*.

5.15 p.m.

Dumanoir, too late, has brought his van squadron down to attack. He is fought off and his rearmost ship, *Neptuno*, is forced to surrender to the *Minotaur* and *Spartiate*.

5.20 p.m.

The last firing ceases as the sun is setting. The *Achille* burns fiercely to the water-line. Many wounded are still aboard. At last the fire reaches the powder magazines. At 5.50 she blows up. An officer on the *Defence* says: "A column of vivid flame shot up to an enormous height in the atmosphere and terminated by expanding into an immense globe . . . a prodigious tree in flames, speckled with many dark spots, . . . the pieces of timber and bodies of men . . . while they were suspended in the clouds."

5.55 p.m.

Admiral Collingwood, who is in command now, comes on board the frigate *Euryalus* and flies his flag.

Over the whole scene of battle, all men, French, Spanish, British, are no longer enemies, but can only help each other.

On nearly every ship, as Jack Nasty-Face records, men "fetch the dead bodies from the after cock-pit, and throw them overboard; these were men . . . taken down to the doctor . . . badly wounded, and who by the time the engagement was ended were dead."

8 p.m.

PARIS, FRANCE

Theatres are crowded. War or no war, Paris is the artistic centre of Europe. "Robinson Crusoe", in three acts, at the Porte-Saint-Martin; the tragedy "Cinna" at the Théâtre Mareux; "Fanchon la veilleuse" at the Vaudeville; "Les trois Sultanes" put on by the *Comédiens Ordinaires* of the Emperor at the Théâtre François, and many others. At the Théâtre Pittoresque, by the Carrefour Gaillon, the second "spectacle", a view of Greenwich, London, has just commenced.

Suddenly, the house lights turn on. At every theatre the manager walks to the front of the stage. The usual chatter of the audience is hushed. He reads an official report, received today by signal telegraph. Napoleon has taken Ulm; 33,000 Austrians are prisoners. France has won a tremendous victory. The final words are drowned in cries of "Vive l'Empereur!" Even aristocrats in their boxes shout, and from the pit people climb the seats, throwing hats in excitement.

Everywhere orchestras strike up the "Marseillaise".

LONDON, ENGLAND

At Astley's Royal Amphitheatre, there opens tonight "*an historical spectacle, as produced in Paris, with original music, called, the DEATH OF CAPTAIN COOK, or the British Columbus, exhibiting the manners . . . combats, of the islanders of O-Why-ee, in the South Sea.*" The Times

Boxes cost 4/–, the gallery 1/–. At 8 p.m., half-way through the show, half-price tickets come on sale. Soldiers with bayonets keep the milling crowd of poorer people in order as they struggle to reach the ticket office. The show will finish at 10 p.m. Audiences love thrills: animals, boats, real water and fire, are all to be seen at Astley's.

WOLVERTON, ENGLAND

A great farm wagon is on the road to Newbury with a load of vetches. Jeremiah Messenger, his wife, and the wagoner are half asleep on the top. In another mile they are due to stop at a wayside inn for the night. The road is empty and silent, except for the creak of the axles. A boy sitting on the shafts has the reins.

The ruts on the road become deeper and the cart lurches more at every turn of the wheels. To the right the road has crumbled: washed away by last week's storms, the ground slopes sharply to a sea of mud.

One of the leading horses stumbles, the others panic, and within seconds the cumbrous, top-heavy wagon crashes over sideways into the morass. The man and woman are crushed in the mud beneath the terrible weight. *The Times* reports their death.

A LONDON STREET

The really poor people have their theatre in the streets. Silliman wrote: "About 10 o'clock at night, I observed one of those little circles . . . the audiences which gather round the ballad singers. These are usually poor women, or little girls . . . of extreme poverty, who collect a few pence by singing ballads at the corners of the streets."

BRIGHTON, ENGLAND

"A select party, as usual, yesterday partook of the delicacies of His Royal Highness's truly hospitable table. Music until 11.20 p.m."
Brighton Weekly Advertiser

The Monday assembly at the Castle Tavern is not its usual glittering self tonight. The Prince is not coming, and many people stay in their lodgings. The 80 by 40-foot ballroom looks a little sad with only 70 people in it. Despite large fires it's none too warm, either. English people like their rooms hot and stuffy. The Master of Ceremonies finds it hard going to stimulate a little gaiety.

A ROAD NEAR SHOREHAM, ENGLAND

Highwaymen have almost disappeared, and modern traffic has yet to come, but roads are dangerous.

"This evening, as Mr. Holt, a quarter-master of the 1st Dragoon Guards, . . . was returning to his station at Arundel (from Brighton), he mistook the road, between the Pad public-house and Lancing, and rode into a deep pool, where he was found dead the next day, with his horse alive by his side, having his head only above the water . . ."
Brighton Weekly Advertiser

THE COUNTRYSIDE

In lonely cottages throughout the forests and moorlands of England, fires are burning of peat, or wood, or coal. Looking into the flames one can forget the hardness of life outside and, in fancy, pass through the smoke-blackened walls to strange lands and things. William Howitt remembers evenings in his boyhood:

"Dr Dally used to make tricks of sleight of hand. . . . One evening in he came with Samuel Davis carrying the yard cock in his hands. . . . The cock made a great cackling and squalling, but Dr Dally, causing someone to hold the cock's head close to the table, took out a piece of chalk, and drew a line from his beak across the table . . . to our amazement he stood stock still, his beak fixed on the line, and seemed bound by a spell. . . . Presently Dr Dally took up the cock and gave it to Sam Davis to take away, when it began to squall as hard as ever.

"Another of his favourite acts . . . was to represent a ship on fire at sea, by floating a lump of camphor on a large basin of water, and setting it on fire, when it floated about in a flame till totally consumed, while he kept . . . talking of it as a real ship; pitying the people on board; asking us where they were to flee to on the wide, wide ocean, where there was no back-door to run out of."

Night

A rising S.W. wind. Heavy seas and swell running westwards. Fleets widely scattered. Some ships have drifted dangerously near the shallows. Battle is over: the fight is against the sea now. Drenched and frozen, sailors are cutting away wreckage, plugging leaks, and high on tottering masts are patching rigging and makeshift yards. Many ships are taken in tow. At 6.15 the *Euryalus* takes the *Revenge*.

Collingwood orders the whole crippled fleet with its prizes, many ships leaking dangerously, to make towards Gibraltar.

Disabled, rolling ships can easily smash into each other. Log of *Euryalus*: "At 7.36 took aback and the *Royal Sovereign* fell on board of our starboard beam, . . . she damaged the main channels, took away the lanyards of the main and mizen rigging, jolly-boat from the quarter and davits, the most of the quarter-deck and waists, . . . took away the main and mizen top-gallant masts, lost the royals and yards. . . . At 7.40 got her clear—made sail on the starboard tack . . ."

Captured ships have British prize-crews in command. On the *Redoutable* the British and French crews, said Captain Lucas afterwards, "spent the whole of that night at the two pumps which were all that remained workable, without, however, being able to keep the water under." On many ships the sea gushes steadily through shattered hulls. Holds are flooded. The wounded, helpless on the lowest decks, are in danger of drowning.

The *Trinidada*, the largest ship in the world, has suffered terribly. An officer from the *Prince* says: "Our first night's work on board the *Trinidada* was to heave the dead overboard, which ammounted to 254 killed." Midshipman Badcock says: "Her beams were covered with Blood, Brains and pieces of Flesh and the after part of her Decks with wounded, some without legs and some without an arm." Perez Galdos says: "Blood ran in streams about the deck . . . and the rolling of the ship carried it hither and thither until it made strange patterns on the planks."

On all ships the moaning of the wounded, of men dying. All night long men struggle against the disasters left by battle.

Ships' logs and journals say:

Entreprenante "saved from the different wrecks 158 men"

Pickle "out boats and saved 150 men"

Naiad "at 10.30 received on board 95 prisoners"

Tonnant "obliged to cut away topmast yards, sails, etc., mainyard, mainsail"

Conqueror "at 10.30 sent a boat with a $7\frac{1}{2}$-inch hawser and a coil of $3\frac{1}{2}$-inch rope, 1 coil of 3-inch for the *Bucentaure*'s stream cable, which we received on board. At 11.30 made sail"

Neptune "at 11 . . . fleet in all directions"

Royal Sovereign "at 12 wore ship, rigged a jury mainmast"

Prince "hauled down fore-topmast staysail to repair shot-holes . . . got fore-runners and tackles forward to secure foremast—cleared away the wreck from the prizes in tow . . . took some Spanish officers on board—came on to blow a hard gale and rain—split the mizen foresail . . . *Trinidada* in tow. . . . Strong gales and rain—saw some of the Fleet at times, very much mauled, and greatest part partly dismasted"

The constant danger of running aground keeps men sounding the depth of water by lead lines.

Log of *Euryalus*: "at 9 sounded in 23 fathoms—made the signal with a gun, Prepare to anchor. . . . At 9.15 sounded in 15 fms. At 9.20 in 14 fms. At 9.35 the water deepened. At 11 sounded in 36 fms. At 11.20 the water shoaled to 26 fms. At 12 in 22 fms. . . . At 12.15 made the signal with three guns to wear, and wore Ship—came to the wind on the larboard tack, head to the westward—*Sovereign* in tow, Fleet and prizes in company"

After

Tomorrow and for three more days a full gale will rage across the whole western Atlantic. Of all the 19 captures, only 4 of the smallest ships will reach Gibraltar. Most of the allied fleet, including the *Fougueux*, *Redoutable* and the *Bucentaure*, will sink or be driven ashore by the storm, to be pounded to pieces on the rocks of Cadiz Bay. The worst wounded will drown. All British ships, even the most damaged, will finally reach England.

Lieutenant John Edwards will see terrible scenes on the magnificent *Trinidada* when it is abandoned to the sea. The Spanish wounded will have to be dropped by rope over the stern. "We had to tie the poor mangled wretches round their waists, or where we could, and lower them into a tumbling boat, some without arms, others no legs, and lacerated all over . . ."

Within ten days British, French, Spanish wounded will fill the hospitals and convents of Cadiz. Wreckage will litter the beaches. An Englishman living in the town wrote: "As far as the eye could reach, the sandy side of the isthmus bordering on the Atlantic was covered with masts and yards, the wreckage of ships. . . . Among others I noticed a topmast marked with the name of the *Swiftsure*, and the broad arrow of England."

For weeks to come, bodies will wash ashore with the tide on the beaches near Cape Trafalgar. They will be buried by Spanish patrols in the sand.

For the living, the people of Cadiz will bring figs, wine and clothing to both friend and foe alike as they are carried on land. The Master of the British *Orion* will find "a carriage . . . backed into the water for him to step into from the boat." A wounded seaman from the *Spartiate* says: "I tried to get up, but I could not, and one of the Spaniards . . . lifted me up in one of the bullock-carts . . . covered me up with one of their great ponchos, and he tapped me on the shoulder, and said 'Bono English!'"

In a week's time Captain Blackwood will be sent to the Governor of Cadiz, under a flag of truce, to arrange an exchange of wounded. He will be entertained to dinner and will bring back wine and fruit for Collingwood.

French prisoners will go to England. Officers will live, on parole, in country lodgings, restricted to one mile's walk on turnpike roads. Senior officers are sometimes allowed in London. Infernet will be loaned £100 by Captain Codrington of the *Orion* and will later

stay as a guest with the Captain's wife. Lucas will be entertained at fashionable parties.

Villeneuve will be sent back to France under an exchange of prisoners. He guesses Napoleon's bitter contempt; his letters remain unanswered. On 21 April he will write to his wife: ". . . I have come to the point when life is a burden and death a duty. . . . Adieu! Adieu!" The next morning he will be found in his Rennes hotel room dead in bed, with six stabs in his chest and a knife driven in to the hilt.

French seamen from Trafalgar will pass the years of the long war, starving on filthy food, herded like cattle in prisons or prison-ships in English harbours. On some ships they will be reduced to fishing in the hold for rats to eat.

On the *Victory*, Nelson's body lies under a sheet. Tomorrow it will be preserved in brandy in a large wooden barrel, placed on end, and brought back to Portsmouth in December.

Lt. Lapenotière will arrive at Falmouth on 4 November in the *Pickle*, carrying Collingwood's Trafalgar dispatches. After 37 hours' fast posting by coach to London he will be at the Admiralty at 1 a.m. on the 6th.

He tells the First Secretary: "Sir, we have gained a great victory, but we have lost Lord Nelson!"

The *London Gazette Extraordinary* is out with the news before breakfast. Guns from the Tower and Hyde Park, church bells, newspapers tell the same story. All England rejoices in Nelson's victory, but mourns his death. Some theatrical shows of grief may be bogus, but most sorrow and tears will be genuine. Perhaps no commander has so captured the imagination of his people.

On 9 January, London will watch his State Funeral.

Today has seen the last sea battle, fought to a finish between rival fleets, in western Europe. A daring but risky use of big ships, and heavy guns, has utterly defeated a resolute enemy in a stronger position. It has been the most decisive victory ever won by the British Navy. It means the end of French sea power under Napoleon. However far the Napoleonic Empire will spread, Britain will always be free to send troops and money to the Continental powers fighting France. Although it is 10 years to Napoleon's final defeat at Waterloo. . . .

Principal Characters in the Story:

AT SEA

Vice-Admiral Horatio Lord Nelson, British Commander-in-Chief, Mediterranean Station.
Vice-Admiral Cuthbert Collingwood, British second-in-command.
Captain Thomas Masterman Hardy, Captain of *Victory*.
Captain Henry Blackwood, Captain of frigate *Euryalus*.
Doctor William Beatty, Surgeon of *Victory*.
First-Lieutenant Pasco, acting as Signal-Lieutenant on *Victory*.
Seaman Jack Nasty-Face, on *Revenge*.
Vice-Admiral Pierre Villeneuve, Commander-in-Chief, Allied Fleet.
Admiral Don Federico Gravina, second-in-command, Allied Fleet.
Captain Jean Lucas, Captain of *Redoubtable*.
Captain Louis Infernet, Captain of *Intrépide*.

ENGLAND

George III, King of England.
George, Prince of Wales.
Admiral Lord Barham, First Lord of the Admiralty.
Emma, Lady Hamilton, mistress to Nelson.
William Howitt, a boy in Yorkshire.
Robert Blincoe, apprentice to a cotton mill.

EUROPE

Napoleon Bonaparte, Emperor of France.
Ludwig van Beethoven, composer.
Benjamin Silliman, American teacher of chemistry, agent for Harvard University.

AFRICA

Mungo Park, doctor, scientist, explorer.

AMERICA

Captain William Clark, soldier and explorer.

NELSON'S TITLE AND RANK AT THE TIME OF HIS DEATH

The Right Honourable Lord Viscount Nelson, Knight of the Bath, Duke of Bronte in Sicily, Knight of the Great Cross of St. Ferdinand and of Merit, Knight of the Order of the Crescent, and of the Illustrious Order of St. Joachim, Vice-Admiral of the White and Commander-in-Chief of His Majesty's Ships and Vessels employed and to be employed in the Mediterranean Station.

HIS DECORATIONS

CHIEF SOURCES USED: (ABBREV. TITLES)

BRITISH MUSEUM, COLINDALE: Newspapers. BRITISH MUSEUM: Journal of Travels, B. Silliman, 1820. Journals of Lewis and Clark, R. G. Thwaites, 1904. Barham Papers, Navy Record Society. Lion Magazine, 1828. The Boy's Country Book, W. Howitt, 1839. Correspondance, Napoleon I, 1858. Nautical Economy, Jack Nasty-Face, 1836. Sporting Magazine, 1805. Correspondence, Collingwood, 1828. State of the Poor, F. M. Eden, 1797. Almanacks, Directories. PUBLIC RECORD OFFICE: Admiralty Minutes, Admiralty Secretary, In Letters and Out Letters. Master's Books, Newgate, Common Side, 1805. BRIGHTON PUBLIC LIBRARY: Newspapers. Almanach de France, 1803. Hist. of Brighton, Erredge. CHELSEA PUBLIC LIBRARY: Descrip. of Chelsea, T. Faulkner, 1829. Trafalgar, J. Corbett, 1910. Nelson's Dispatches and Letters, H. Nicolas, 1844. Naval Hist., W. James, 1826. Death of Nelson, W. Beatty, 1807. Enemy at Trafalgar, E. Fraser, 1906. Sailors, E. Fraser, 1913. H.M.S. Victory, K. Fenwick, 1959, Cassell. HORNSEY PUBLIC LIBRARY: MIDDLESEX, C. 1820.

The author wishes to thank, for his help and advice, the Commanding Officer, H.M.S. *Victory* (Ship), Portsmouth.

A NOTE ABOUT BRITISH MONEY:

	U.S. EQUIVALENT TODAY
1d (one *penny*)	1¢
12d (twelve pennies or pence) = 1s (one *shilling*)	12¢
2s + 6d (two *shillings* and six *pence*, written 2/6) = 1 half crown	30¢
20s (twenty *shillings*) = £1 (one *pound*)	$2.40
£1 + 1s (one *pound* and one *shilling*) = 1 gn (one *guinea*)	$2.52
Example: in 1805 a seaman's monthly wage was £1/9/6d (one *pound*, nine *shillings* and six *pence*)	$3.54